Post-Democracy After the Crises

To the memory of Alessandro Pizzorno (01/01/1924–04/04/2019), who, in 1973, enabled me to embark on a career of research on comparative European industrial relations; who, in 1995, welcomed me to Florence and the European University Institute; who, in 2002, interested Giuseppe Laterza in my Fabian Society pamphlet, *Coping with Post-Democracy*, which led to my writing, in 2003, *Post-Democracy*.

Post-Democracy After the Crises

Colin Crouch

polity

Copyright © Colin Crouch 2020

The right of Colin Crouch to be identified as Author of this Work has been asserted in accordance with the UK Copyright, Designs and Patents Act 1988.

First published in 2020 by Polity Press

Polity Press
65 Bridge Street
Cambridge CB2 1UR, UK

Polity Press
101 Station Landing
Suite 300
Medford, MA 02155, USA

All rights reserved. Except for the quotation of short passages for the purpose of criticism and review, no part of this publication may be reproduced, stored in a retrieval system or transmitted, in any form or by any means, electronic, mechanical, photocopying, recording or otherwise, without the prior permission of the publisher.

ISBN-13: 978-1-5095-4156-0
ISBN-13: 978-1-5095-4157-7 (pb)

A catalogue record for this book is available from the British Library.

Library of Congress Cataloging-in-Publication Data
Names: Crouch, Colin, 1944- author.
Title: Post-democracy after the crises / Colin Crouch.
Description: Cambridge, UK ; Medford, MA : Polity, 2020. | Includes bibliographical references and index. | Summary: "Crouch's provocative argument in Post-Democracy has in many ways been vindicated by recent events, but these have also highlighted some weaknesses of the original thesis and shown that the situation today is even worse"-- Provided by publisher.
Identifiers: LCCN 2019033304 (print) | LCCN 2019033305 (ebook) | ISBN 9781509541560 (hardback) | ISBN 9781509541577 (paperback) | ISBN 9781509541584 (epub)
Subjects: LCSH: Democracy--Philosophy. | World politics--21st century.
Classification: LCC JC423 .C7673 2020 (print) | LCC JC423 (ebook) | DDC 321.8--dc23
LC record available at https://lccn.loc.gov/2019033304
LC ebook record available at https://lccn.loc.gov/2019033305

Typeset in 11 on 13pt Sabon
by Fakenham Prepress Solutions, Fakenham, Norfolk NR21 8NL
Printed and bound in Great Britain by TJ International Limited

The publisher has used its best endeavours to ensure that the URLs for external websites referred to in this book are correct and active at the time of going to press. However, the publisher has no responsibility for the websites and can make no guarantee that a site will remain live or that the content is or will remain appropriate.

Every effort has been made to trace all copyright holders, but if any have been overlooked the publisher will be pleased to include any necessary credits in any subsequent reprint or edition.

For further information on Polity, visit our website:
politybooks.com

Contents

Acknowledgements vi

Abbreviations vii

Preface ix

1 What Is Post-Democracy? 1

2 Inequality and Corruption 19

3 The 2008 Financial Crisis 41

4 The European Debt Crisis 66

5 Politicized Pessimistic Nostalgia: A Cure Worse than the Disease 91

6 The Fate of Twentieth-Century Political Identities 118

7 Beyond Post-Democracy? 139

References 167

Index 173

Acknowledgements

My wife, Joan, has, as always, been an unfailing partner in developing arguments and ideas, and in reading successive drafts.

From the initial writing of *Post-Democracy* in 2003 to this current volume, I have enjoyed invaluable encouragement and support from Giuseppe Laterza.

I have benefited greatly from discussions and seminars with Donatella Della Porta, Mario Pianta and their colleagues and students at the Scuola Normale Superiore, Florence, where I was a visiting professor during 2018.

Abbreviations

BBC	British Broadcasting Corporation
BCBS	Basel Committee on Banking Supervision
EC	European Commission
ECB	European Central Bank
ECJ	European Court of Justice
EEC	European Economic Community
ERM	Exchange Rate Mechanism
EU	European Union
FAA	Federal Aviation Authority (US)
FN	Front National (France)
FPÖ	Freiheitliche Partei Österreichs (Austria)
GATT	General Agreement on Tariffs and Trade
GDP	gross domestic product
IIF	International Institute for Finance
IMF	International Monetary Fund
IT	information technology
LTCM	Long-Term Capital Management
M5S	Movimento Cinque Stelle
NATO	North Atlantic Treaty Organization
NPM	New Public Management
OECD	Organization for Economic Cooperation and Development

	Abbreviations
ÖVP	Österreichische Volkspartei (Austria)
PiS	Prawo i Sprawiedliwość (Poland)
SVP	Schweizerische Volkspartei (Switzerland)
UK	United Kingdom
US	United States
USSR	Union of Soviet Socialist Republics
WTO	World Trade Organization

Preface

In my book *Post-Democracy*, first published in 2003, I argued that in much of the western world we were drifting towards a condition where democracy was becoming a shadow of itself. Its institutions and habits remained: contested elections took place; governments could be brought down and peacefully replaced; political debate seemed fierce. But its vivacity and vigour had declined: parties and governments did not so much respond to desires articulated autonomously by groups of citizens, but manipulated issues and public opinion. Meanwhile, the real energy of the political system had passed into the hands of small elites of politicians and the corporate rich, who increasingly ensured that politics responded to the wishes of the latter. No one was to 'blame' for this in the normal sense, even those who gained from it. The two principal causes were beyond easy human manipulation. First, globalization had removed major economic decisions to levels that could not be reached from where democracy was concentrated: the nation-state. This was rendering much political economic debate futile. Second, the divisions of class and religion that had once enabled ordinary citizens to acquire a political identity were losing their meaning, making it increasingly difficult for us all to answer the question: 'Who am I, politically?' And unless we can answer that question, it is difficult for us to play an active part in democracy.

Because of these major forces of change, the worlds of politics and of normal life were drifting apart. Politicians responded to this by resorting to increasingly artificial means of communication with voters, using the techniques of advertising and market research in a very one-sided kind of interaction. Voters were becoming like puppets, dancing to tunes set by the manipulators of public opinion, rarely able to articulate their own concerns and priorities. This only intensified the growing artificiality of democracy; hence, post-democracy. I did not argue in 2003 that we had already reached a state of post-democracy. Most contemporary societies with long-established democratic institutions still had many citizens capable of making new demands and frustrating the plans of the puppet-masters; but we were on the road towards it.

I made three important mistakes in this account. First, I concentrated too much on the importance of what I called 'democratic moments', points in time when political professionals lost control of the agenda, permitting groups of citizens to shape it. I did not pay attention to the institutions that sustain and protect democracy outside those moments. Second, although I recognized xenophobic populism as one of the movements in contemporary society that seemed to challenge post-democracy, I both underestimated its depth and importance, and did not see how it would mark more an intensification of post-democratic trends than an answer to them. Third, I talked of both the failure of the middle and lower social classes of post-industrial societies to develop a distinctive politics, and the important role of feminism as another challenge to post-democracy, but failed to perceive that some elements of feminism are in part the distinctive politics of those classes.

These mistakes are linked. In the initial years of this century it seemed possible to take for granted the viability of the constitutional order that safeguards democracy – and indeed disguises post-democracy as democracy. The xenophobic movements that have achieved such prominence since that time in Europe, the USA and elsewhere have made it clear that they do not accept the priority of such institutions as the autonomy of the judiciary, the rule of law or the role of parliaments. Since these movements stand predominantly on the political right, it tends today to be parties of the centre and left that defend these institutions. In a longer historical perspective it may seem strange that the left is defending constitutions against a right that has always claimed to have that role; that is a mark of how politics is changing. Further, xenophobic movements are becoming the main bearers, not just of fear and hatred of foreigners, but of a pessimistic, nostalgic social conservatism in general, including resentment at recent advances made by women. Movements guided at least in part by feminist ideas then become their major antagonists, going beyond 'women's issues' as such. I hope by the end of this book to have remedied these mistakes.

Post-Democracy also appears not so much in error, as dated, for other reasons. It began with an account of the taken-for-granted complacency that surrounded democracy in many parts of the world at its time of writing. This was the period when Francis Fukuyama's celebration of liberal capitalist democracy as the summit of human institutional achievement, *The End of History and the Last Man* (1992), was still in vogue. It was several years before books were to appear with titles like the late Peter Mair's *The Hollowing of Western Democracy* (2013), but it was in 2018 that such a literature became a flood, with David Runciman's *How Democracy Ends*, Daniel Ziblatt and Steven Levitsky's *How Democracies Die*, Robert Kuttner's *Can Democracy Survive Global Capitalism?* and Nancy MacLean's *Democracy in Chains*. The annual democracy index produced by the Economist Intelligence Unit considered that 13 per cent of the world's population lived in 'fully functioning' democracies in 2006

– the first year in which the report was published. By 2017 it had dropped to 4.5 per cent (Economist Intelligence Unit, annual).

I was also writing before the financial crisis of 2008 was to demonstrate one of my core arguments: that lobbying for the interests of global business had produced a deregulated economy that neglected all other interests in society. I had not fully appreciated the special place of the financial sector in the array of capitalist interests, and the particular challenge it presented to democracy. Two years later the European debt crisis seemed to produce perfect examples of post-democracy in action, as parliaments in Greece and Italy were presented with a choice: vote for the appointment of prime ministers designated by the International Monetary Fund, the European Central Bank, the European Commission and an unofficial committee of leading banks, or receive no help out of the crisis. The forms of democratic choice were preserved: the new prime ministers – both of whom had formerly been employees of Goldman Sachs, one of the banks at the heart of the crises – were not simply imposed; parliaments had to vote for them. That is how post-democracy works. But that account is itself over-simple. There are serious questions over the democratic credentials of the previous governments of both countries.

Finally, the years since I wrote *Post-Democracy* have seen the extraordinary rise of social media and their use in political mobilization. In my book, I welcomed the role of the Internet as enabling civil society groups to organize and spread discussions, providing some useful countervailing power against large corporations and media organizations. This we now know was naive. Since the early years of the century, the Internet economy has produced its own colossal enterprises, compounding further the potential political role of capitalist power and wealth. The Internet has also facilitated the distribution of extraordinary outbursts of hate speech, a deterioration in the quality of debate and a capacity to broadcast falsehood. Much of this is linked to the rise of the new xenophobic movements of the far right, the self-styled 'alt.right'. Social media do continue to enable civil society groups and individuals who previously lacked any chance of political voice to find one, but the possessors of colossal wealth have been purchasing technology and expertise that enable them to discover the salient characteristics of millions of citizens and target them with vast numbers of persuasive messages, giving the impression of huge movements of opinion, apparently coming from millions of separate people, that in fact emanate from a single source. It is difficult to imagine a more perfectly post-democratic form of politics, giving an impression of debate and conflict that is really stage-managed from a small number of concealed sources. What seemed to be a liberating, democratizing technology has turned out to favour a small number of extremely rich individuals and groups – those wealthy persons having the temerity to pose as the opponents of 'elites'. The relationship of social media to democracy and post-democracy requires a re-examination.

These various developments make necessary the revision, updating and changing of the arguments in *Post-Democracy*. In Chapter 1 of *Post-Democracy After the Crises*, I restate what I meant by the idea in the first place and why it seemed relevant to write about it. Chapters 2–6 deal in turn with the forces that seem to be exacerbating post-democratic trends: the corruption of politics by wealth and lobbying power; the financial crisis and the conduct of measures to end it; the European debt crisis; the rise of xenophobic populism; and the erosion of democracy's roots among citizens. *Post-Democracy* was a dystopia. A dystopia says: this is the direction in which we are heading, and it seems bad. But if the author wants to avoid bleak pessimism, she or he must also say to the reader: if you do not like where we are heading, here are some things we can do about it. Chapter 7 tries to do what was attempted in the final chapter of *Post-Democracy*, 'Where Do We Go from Here?', but the mood as well as some of the substantive ideas are different.

Post-Democracy was based on a pamphlet I wrote in 2002 for the Fabian Society, entitled *Coping with Post-Democracy*. Most Fabian pamphlets are addressed to policymakers and tell them what they should do to tackle various problems. But policymakers themselves constituted an important part of the problem that I was discussing. I therefore addressed ordinary citizens who stood little chance of doing anything about the major social, political and economic forces standing behind the development. They could, however, work out how to cope with it, alleviating its impact on their lives. Post-democracy as I saw it was a disappointing and worrying process, but it was not frightening; it could be 'coped with'. The situation today is worse. Not only are the main new weapons of civil society, those of information technology, being turned against it, but in the settled democracies of the world we are confronting important challenges to constitutional order and a resurgence of xenophobia, almost all coming from the far right. Although these challenges are not as extreme as the fascist and Nazi movements of the interwar years, they are part of the same political family, and raise concerns for everyone from the centre right to the left – except that part of the far left that is beginning to share some of the far right's rhetoric. If this is where post-democracy has now brought us, 'coping' is too complacent. Confrontation is necessary.

Post scriptum

The text of this book was completed before Boris Johnson formed a minority Conservative government in the UK in the late summer of 2019. This alone explains the absence of examples drawn from that government's experience to illustrate some central themes in Chapter 4, including relations between xenophobic populist movements and the judiciary, their creation of 'alternative facts', and the implicit encouragement of intolerance towards opponents.

1
What Is Post-Democracy?

Recent general election campaigns in the United Kingdom have presented a visual image of what I mean by post-democracy that is more expressive than many words – and I expect the same images are prominent in other mature democracies too. A politician appears on the television news making a speech, surrounded by enthusiastic supporters, carefully balanced for all ages and races and both genders, waving placards bearing slogans of the party in question. It has all the marks of a politician embedded in the people, who are demonstrating their spontaneous excitement. But the placards have all been produced by a central source, not autonomously by those holding them. Sometimes the mischievous camera pans back to reveal that the politician and the little group of supporters are actually standing alone, together with a few media representatives, in a corner of a large, empty warehouse. There is no larger audience; this is not a public meeting. These gatherings are held in different cities, politicians being required to travel vast distances in order to show that they cover the country in their determination to meet the people. But the warehouses are nearly always on the edge of a city, around ring roads and motorway approaches where virtually nobody ever goes. For reasons of security, traffic congestion and fears of encountering hostile citizens, these election rallies rarely approach a population. All the trappings of democratic encounters are there: all parts of the country are visited; the politicians stand among highly diverse groups of persons, not isolated on a platform; they make strong and emotional appeals. But the event is as empty of serious encounter as are the warehouses in which they are staged.

The idea of 'post-' is very frequently used today: post-industrial, post-modern, post-liberal, post-ironic. This suggests a society that knows where it has been and what it is ceasing to be, but not where it is going. However, it can also mean something very precise. Essential to 'post-' is the idea of a parabola through which the phenomenon in question passes over time. The general idea is depicted in Figure 1.1. After its initial appearance, it grows in significance, eventually reaching a peak, after which it subsides in importance. Its importance 'score' eventually seems no higher than in its early years, but accumulations over time do not easily disappear. Their mark is left in memories and, more importantly, in institutions that were created by the phenomenon during its dominant period and that, at least for a time, are not abolished. For this reason, the situation after, say, 70 years is not the same as at year 0. Let us take the case of 'post-industrialism', a phenomenon that can be measured fairly clearly as either the proportion of gross domestic product (GDP) or the proportion of employment accounted for by manufacturing industry. This first rose from low levels during early industrialization, reached a peak (in most western economies during the 1970s), and then declined. Today its level resembles that of industrialism's earlier years. But this does not mean that we are reverting to being 'pre-industrial' or 'non-industrial'. The accumulations of industrialism and their impact on our lives are still with us; we have become 'post-industrial'.

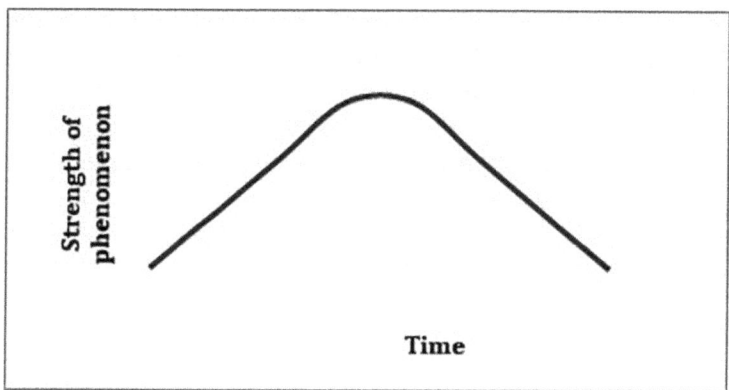

Figure 1.1 The parabola: from pre- to post- in the life of a phenomenon

A similar point applies to democracy. The fact that, as I argue below, democracy has lost strength in recent decades does not mean that we are living in pre- or non-democratic societies. The achievements of the democratic period have left a major legacy of practices, attitudes, values and institutions. These are still active. This gives ground for optimism, but it also explains something important about post-democracy: we do not notice that democracy has weakened, because its institutions and habits remain; but the real energy of the political system has passed into the hands of small elites of politicians and the corporate rich, who increasingly ensure that politics responds to their wishes.

In a criticism of my concept, Stephen Welch argued in *Hyperdemocracy* (2013) that rather than a decline of democracy, we are today trying to have too much of it, politicizing issues that are inappropriate for such treatment. But he and I are talking about two sides of the same coin. I would reconcile our positions by pointing out that when political debate is about nothing, it tries to be about everything. When there is very little real debate over major policy directions (a fundamental characteristic of post-democracy), politicians start exploring every little avenue they can in order to claim that they have found a difference from their opponents – anything from each other's personal morality to the desirability of particular medical treatments or ways of teaching children to read. This leads to an intrusion of politics – whether democratic or not – into areas with which it is not well equipped to deal.

To sustain my argument that changes in our political life can be described as steps on a road towards post-democracy, I need to demonstrate two things: first, that there was a period in the recent past when democracy could be said to have been strong; and second, that there has been a falling away since. The first requires identification of a 'democratic moment'.

Democratic Moments

Democracy thrives when there are major opportunities for the mass of ordinary people to participate, through discussion and autonomous organizations, in shaping the agenda of public life, and when they are actively using these opportunities. This is ambitious, an ideal model, which can almost never be fully achieved; but, like all impossible ideals, it sets a marker. It is intensely practical to consider where our conduct stands in relation to an ideal, since in that way we can try to improve. It is essential to take this approach to democracy rather than the more common one, which is to scale down definitions of the ideal so that they conform to what we actually achieve. That way lies complacency, self-congratulation and an absence of concern to identify ways in which democracy is being weakened.

Societies probably come closest to democracy in my maximal sense in the early years of achieving it or after great regime crises, when enthusiasm for democracy is widespread and concern for political developments intense, as people feel their lives are being touched by them; when many diverse groups and organizations of ordinary people share in the task of trying to frame a political agenda that will at last respond to their concerns; when the powerful interests that dominate undemocratic societies are wrong-footed and thrown on the defensive; and when the political system has not quite discovered how to manage and manipulate the new demands. These are democratic moments.

In most of western Europe and North America, we had major democratic moments at some point between the 1930s (in the United States and Scandinavia) and the years immediately following the Second World War (the rest of us). Until those points, few countries had had extensive periods of full male adult suffrage – in even fewer did women enjoy political citizenship. Masses of ordinary people then discovered they had a political voice, and formed parties and other organizations to express their concerns. There had been earlier rumblings of democratic moments, especially around the turn of the century and the time of the First World War, but in several European societies the elites who had been accustomed to having political life serve their interests alone were simply not prepared to accept this invasion of their privileged space. Many of them threw their weight behind fascist and Nazi parties, which, despite speaking a populist rhetoric and making use of mass mobilizations, were deeply hostile to democracy and, once in power, suppressed it with ruthless violence. The defeat of Adolf Hitler, Benito Mussolini and other fascist leaders in the Second World War and the devastation of their countries led these elites to accept not only the election of governments, but also the pursuit of political agendas promoted by groups from outside their own ranks.

We see this most clearly in the themes that the social democratic and socialist left had been trying to bring to the table since the late nineteenth century: workers' rights, a welfare state, free or heavily subsidized education and health services, redistributive taxation. But it was not only the left that now adopted these policies. One can, for example, see the impact of democracy on the politics of Roman Catholicism. The church had set its face against all dilutions of aristocratic and other forms of elite rule ever since the French Revolution, and in the twentieth century had supported the fascist suppression of infant democracies in Italy, Portugal and Spain. There was however a Christian democratic wing to Catholic politics, struggling against the prevailing authoritarianism. After the Second World War, this moved from being marginalized by Catholic elites to become the dominant form of Christian politics, for several decades being the most successful group of parties in western Europe. This was all part of the democratic moment.

The Weakening of Democracy

Some entropy of maximal democracy has to be expected, but two primary factors, in turn producing a third, have accelerated the process. These are:

- economic globalization and the associated rise of the giant firm;
- changes in class structure and (in western Europe but not the US) a decline in the power of religion, which have more or less inevitably weakened the main forces that linked ordinary people to political life;
- and, in consequence of these two forces, a growing tendency for politicians to reduce their links with their mass supporters and prefer the company of global business elites.

Globalization has weakened democracy in two ways. First, it has reduced the reach of national governments. If the most important decisions that shape the economic world take place at global levels, while democracy remains rooted in nation-states, inevitably much democratic activity can come to seem pointless. Second, the institutions that have been most advanced by globalization are transnational corporations, which have outgrown the governance capacity of individual nation-states. If they do not like the regulatory or fiscal regime in one country, they threaten to move to another, and increasingly states compete in their willingness to offer them favourable conditions and tax regimes, as they need the investment. Democracy has simply not kept pace with capitalism's rush to the global. The best it can manage are certain international groupings of states, but even the most important by far of these, the European Union (EU), is a clumsy pygmy in relation to the agile corporate giants, and its own democratic quality, while far stronger than anything similar in the world, is weak.

Today's dominant politico-economic ideology, neoliberalism, has turned this weakening of the nation-state into a virtue. If it is believed that governments are almost by definition incompetent and that large firms are necessarily efficient, then the less power the former have and the more freedom from them that firms gain, the better. Large numbers of politicians and politically active persons, from all points of the political spectrum, came to believe this during the latter years of the twentieth century. A decline in the importance of political democracy was almost bound to follow.

The second factor has been quite different. Class and religion were the main forces that enabled ordinary, non-political people to acquire political identities. As will be discussed in more depth in Chapter 6, this happened because class and often religious identity put people on different sides in struggles for entry into political citizenship. These class and religious identities were attributes that people well understood. When they acquired political meaning through these struggles, people could understand which parties were working for or against 'people like them', and could vote accordingly. Once universal adult suffrage had been achieved, these struggles gradually passed from being remembered experience to being something learned from parents and grandparents about the past. Meanwhile, the new classes being created by the growth of post-industrial occupations did not face struggles for admission to citizenship, and therefore have not carried clues to political identity. Similarly, as European societies became secularized and religious leaders departed from their traditional conservative political positions, adherence to a particular faith – or none – also ceased to convey political identity.

Most adults have continued to vote, though turnout has slowly declined almost everywhere, and voting has become an act rather detached from life's deeply felt activities. Figure 1.2 shows changes in the proportion of persons qualified to vote in national parliamentary elections who actually did so across the main west European countries between the mid-1980s and the most recent election (as of mid-2019). Such a comparison between two periods of time conceals fluctuations that might have

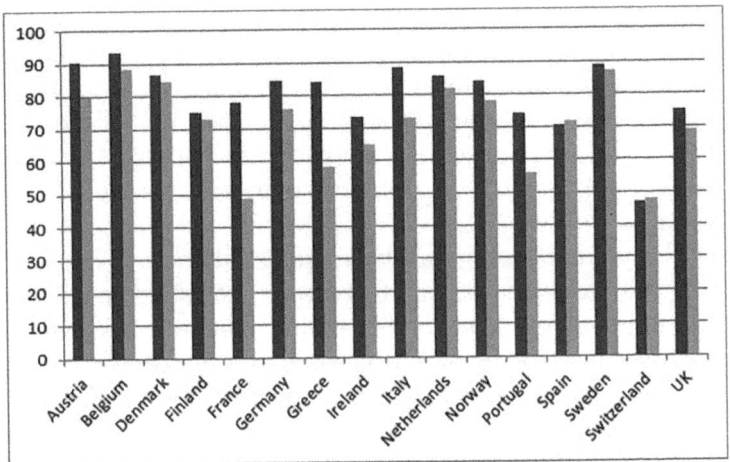

NB: 'Germany' in the mid-1980s was the German Federal Republic; today it is united Germany

Figure 1.2 Turnout in national parliamentary elections, mid-1980s (dark grey) and late 2010s (light grey), west European countries

Source: Author's calculations based on Wikipedia data

What Is Post-Democracy?

taken place between them, and cannot cope with special factors affecting individual countries at those two periods themselves. However, it is clear that everywhere except Switzerland (where turnout has in any case always been low) and (marginally) Spain, there has been decline. In some cases this has been minor, but in others it has been strong. Two countries (Belgium and Italy) moved from compulsory voting during the period, but that seemed to have little impact on the general trend in voting.

With the exception of Slovenia, the populations of central and eastern Europe did not respond with exceptional enthusiasm to being able to vote in free elections after the fall of communism, turnout in their first elections during the 1990s being typically lower than those found even now in most of western Europe. Since then, there have been varying patterns (Figure 1.3), but decline has predominated.

The mass memberships of parties themselves also often declined, leaving their smaller number of activists representing the traditional symbolic identities of the classes

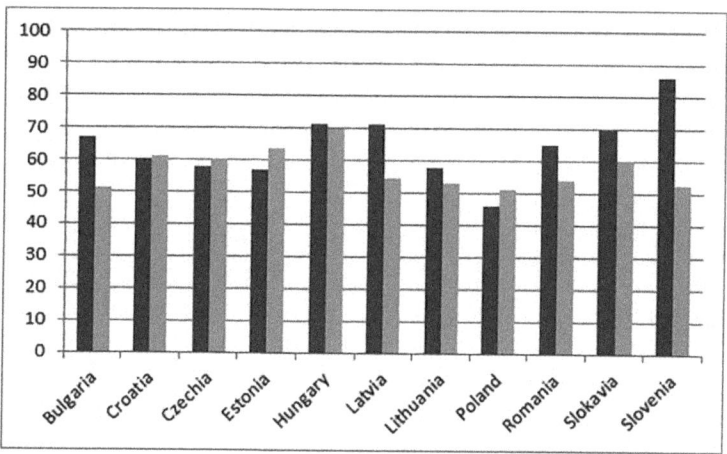

Figure 1.3 Turnout in national parliamentary elections, early 1990s (dark grey) and late 2010s (light grey), central European EU member states

Source: Author's calculations based on Wikipedia data

and faiths that had built the party but not extending into new parts of the population. Party leaderships observed this, which meant that the mass parties were declining in their value to leaders as ways of connecting them to voters at large. As core constituencies shrank, party leaders came increasingly to believe that they did not really need core constituencies. Rather, they wanted to be able to take them for granted as voters who had no other home to which they could go, leaving leaders free to find votes across as wide a range of opinion as possible. This necessarily meant a decline in the clarity of parties' profiles, weakening further any strong bonds they might have with citizens.

Parties increasingly sought to relate to voters through the techniques of market research and advertising. Policies and party images became like goods being sold in a market to mass consumers, where firms have no direct knowledge of potential customers as people, but only as purchasing units identified in surveys, focus groups and trial marketing campaigns. Politicians ceased to be people who represented various social categories because of their close contacts with them as fellow citizens, but a separate political class, the recipients of professional marketing data about customer-electors. Socially, they would increasingly prefer to mix with the leaders of global corporations, whose investments they wanted to lure to their economies, and whose funds they wanted to finance their increasingly expensive election campaigns.

Taken together, these processes generated a spiral of increasing remoteness of political leaders from electorates. The apotheosis of this change was Silvio Berlusconi in Italy. The main parties of the Italian centre right and centre left had collapsed in the early 1990s in a wave of corruption scandals that provoked a brief democratic moment of anger. The communist party, by now a moderate one, was left as the only major organized political force in the country. Berlusconi was the country's richest entrepreneur, owning businesses across the post-industrial spectrum from football to financial services, television stations to supermarkets (Mancini 2011). He had been politically associated with the now defunct socialist party, and had a range of legal cases for corruption hanging over his head. Despite these strong links to the old regime, he appeared on the political scene as an outsider who would clean up the system and, most important, provide an alternative to the communist party, which many Italians still feared.

Berlusconi rapidly created a major, winning national political party, called Forza Italia (a politically meaningless phrase, derived from a football slogan), using, not a membership base, but the financial and personnel resources of his enterprises and his ownership of major television and print media networks. The phenomenon became known as a *partito impresa*, a corporation party. Over subsequent years, Forza Italia developed a membership base and began to resemble a normal party, collapsing along with other established parties during the 2010s under a new wave of populism. However, its initial circumstances followed a post-democratic model of having few connections to voters and no historical social roots.

In 2003, I did not argue that in the western world we had already arrived at a state of post-democracy. That would happen if we were in societies in which no spontaneous movements could arise from the general population to give a shock to the political system. Our societies were clearly still able to do this. Three movements in particular had been doing so, bringing to the political agenda issues that established elites would sooner have done without: feminism, environmentalism and xenophobia. The developments I had identified had set us on the road to post-democracy, but we were not yet there.

Liberal Democracy and Other Forms

My argument took for granted that democracy was representative, liberal democracy. This is not the only form. Democracy can be direct, with all citizens participating in making decisions rather than electing representatives. This is possible in small groups, deciding on issues that are readily understood, and there are many examples of it around the world. If direct democracy is attempted among large populations, it takes the form of referenda. Here issues, however complex in themselves, have to be simplified into a binary choice: one is either for or against a particular proposal. If the question is very precise and voters can be expected to be fully conversant with it, this can work quite effectively and gives citizens important opportunities directly to shape their environment. If these conditions are not fulfilled, there is a risk that voters will use a referendum as a chance to air their general dissatisfactions; nothing forces them to vote according to the question asked. When the then Italian prime minister, Matteo Renzi, called a referendum in December 2016 on a somewhat abstruse question of constitutional reform, he was surprised to find that his opponents turned the campaign into a general vote of confidence in him – which he lost, and so resigned. When in the same year the British people were invited to vote on whether they wanted their country to remain in the EU, researchers found that many voted to leave in order to express a protest vote about various things that they did not like – the EU being only partly related to them.

It has been difficult to improve on representational democracy, whereby we vote for members of a parliament or other deliberative assembly, who then in turn support or oppose a government formed from among them, processing issues, making decisions and passing laws on a daily basis. This is by no means a perfect solution. What does it mean to be able to choose an individual as a 'representative', especially in a mass situation where one is virtually certain not to know at all the person concerned? In practice, this problem has been resolved by candidates standing for particular parties, the general programmes of which we might be expected to know more about. This still runs into the problem mentioned above and to be discussed in more detail in Chapter 6: by what means do citizens come to see particular parties as representing them? There is no satisfactory theoretical answer to that question; it depends on historical chance and various sociological conditions. In the absence of strong two-way flows of interaction between parties and citizens, there is no way to ensure that representative democracy 'works', and commentators should be more honest than they usually are in recognizing that.

The idea of liberal democracy is related to that of representation, but the two things are by no means the same. Liberalism as most broadly conceived means acceptance that human knowledge is fundamentally uncertain, and that even firmly held beliefs might prove to be wrong. Liberalism is therefore tolerant of diversity and of approaches with which one is not personally sympathetic, because one can never be certain that knowledge and understanding will not change. Liberals are entitled to be intolerant of intolerance and of unquestioned beliefs, but not of much else. They might hold religious or political beliefs themselves, but they will never be so convinced that theirs are correct that they have a right to suppress those holding different ones. In economic terms they have a general preference for markets over central state planning, as the former contain more possibilities for flexibility and adjustment. Science is, or should be, liberal, in the sense that, while knowledge has to be accepted and used, one must always be ready for currently accepted truths to be found wrong or at least capable of being improved on. Liberalism rejects the imposition from above of unchallenged rule; it insists on debate and the constant possibility of challenge to authority. Of course, from time to time irreversible decisions have to be made, and the risk taken that they will prove to have been poor ones. But the scope for revision and changing views must be maintained as much as possible. For example, an irreversible decision may have to be taken to build a new motorway; but general road-building strategy for the future must continue to be discussed. It is fundamental to liberalism that no governing regimes are permanent. There must always be debate, and the certainty of new elections every few years. Today's minority must stand a chance of becoming tomorrow's majority; a party in government today must see a serious possibility in not being the government tomorrow, and therefore must want to share a cross-party value consensus in keeping competition open and fair.

As Adrian Pabst (2016) has noted, in a critique of the idea of post-democracy, there must also be institutions that stand outside the reach of democracy itself, able to check the misuse of power by elected rulers. This reflects the liberal view that political leaders, even democratically elected ones, are vulnerable to various kinds of corruption, in particular to aggrandizing their own power and using it to manipulate events and apparent facts to guarantee that they keep winning elections and stay in office. In the famous words of Lord Acton, a nineteenth-century British Liberal politician, 'all power corrupts; absolute power corrupts absolutely'. In short, liberal democracy refers to a form of government that combines universal adult citizenship and voting rights with institutions that entrench the protection of uncertainty, diversity and the possibility of change, even against the preferences of those who win democratic elections. It is particularly important that law courts and the judiciary remain beyond the reach of political interference, and that government remains subordinate to the law, what Germans call the *Rechtstaat* (literally, 'law state'). The achievement of the rule of law predates the rise of democracy, and there is occasionally tension between the two principles. From time to time, elected politicians claim that 'unelected judges' should be subordinate to them. This is a major warning sign that politicians are hungry for 'absolute power'. We shall encounter several recent examples in the following chapters.

Liberal democracy has its enemies. There are those who believe in the imposition from above of clear rules by rulers who know best. Monarchs and monarchists were once the primary exponents of that view – 'monarch' means 'rule by one'. Religious organizations are often governed in this way, both internally and in what they try to impose on the rest of society. Nearly all modern business leaders are enemies of liberal democracy within their own organizations, insisting on the unchallengeable authority of the chief executive officer, and they sometimes believe that the same principles should be applied more widely; if ordinary employees (citizens) have no right to a voice, decisions can be made quickly and firmly. It is often believed that the efficiency and profit that this brings amply compensate for many people's views being ridden over roughshod or not even heard, and for occasional major errors. Such persons will often be heard comparing favourably the Chinese state's ability to build airports wherever and whenever it likes, while in western countries people who would be negatively affected are allowed to argue their case and at least hold up progress while their objections are considered.

Historically, opposition to liberal democracy was a position of the traditional conservative right and then of the fascistic authoritarian right, and, as we shall see in Chapter 5, this opposition is enjoying a major revival today. But for much of the twentieth century the major challenge came from the left, in the state-socialist or communist form of 'people's democracy'. That phrase had been adopted by the victors of the Russian Revolution, later exported to those parts of Europe in which the Russian army was in occupation after the defeat of fascism and Nazism in the Second World War. It was also used in the separate communist revolution in Yugoslavia and in many parts of the developing world as revolutionary elites threw off colonial rule by west European powers. Communism was an example of the eruption of politics relevant to the lives of working people, and the elevation of the working class as a heroic class. But its democratic moment was very brief. According to the theories of Karl

Marx and of Vladimir Lenin, the interests of the working class were not those actually voiced by working people themselves, but by those who would fulfil the historical destiny of that class, as outlined in Marx's writings. The vast majority of workers could not be expected to grasp this, so the key role in interpreting their interests was given to the communist parties that represented them. There being a grave danger that enemies of the revolution might subvert this process, power had to be kept in the hands of a reliable leadership. Debate, dissent and the presentation of alternatives were all crushed. Particularly when Josef Stalin assumed total power in the Soviet Union, as Russia and the neighbouring countries absorbed into its regime became known, this intolerance unleashed a reign of terror and violence as vicious as that of Nazism.

Europe's communist regimes never developed the climate of open debate and ability to criticize governments without being punished that are the vital substructure of democracy. They eventually collapsed in 1990 as soon as a new reform leadership in Moscow made it clear that Russian tanks would no longer be available to crush opponents. Whereas institutions in the western world, built on liberal political and economic principles that incorporate uncertainty and constant needs to change, have been able to adapt to challenges, the rigid and hierarchical certainties of state socialism collapsed entirely once they were no longer guaranteed by armed force.

The record of state socialist regimes almost everywhere suggests that Acton's dictum applies just as much to their leaders as to others. Since the fall of Russian and east European state socialism in 1990, few have been willing to argue for the superiority of people's democracy. For present purposes, this leaves us with two main lessons. First, those institutions that sustain the liberal version of democracy are highly important, even though they also play a role in sustaining post-democracy. Second, the problem of the corruption of liberal democracy by wealth remains. We shall return to both these themes in later chapters.

What Is Post-Democracy?

The history of people's democracy from the Russian Revolution to the collapse of the system in 1990 cannot be considered a case of the parabola of democracy, as it provided no accretion of democratic practice and institutions. Dictatorship and the persecution of opponents had settled in by the mid-1920s, and from the outset in those countries where state socialism was imposed by the Russian army after 1945. We see this legacy in the difficulty experienced by countries in the Soviet bloc in establishing democratic institutions after 1990. In Russia and its immediate neighbours, they remain very fragile if they exist at all, and state power is routinely exercised to silence opponents. Those countries further west that have joined the EU have fared better, though there has been considerable difficulty in establishing stable party systems and there are important lurches towards authoritarianism. Again, we shall return to these themes in later chapters.

Post-democracy can be said to occur only where there is a history of reasonably strong democracy, leaving behind a legacy of practices and institutions, which, while extremely valuable, by their continued presence create the impression that all is well. Post-democracy refers to a weariness with the obligations of political citizenship, alongside a complacent belief that democracy is in safe enough hands and barely needs to be practised. A striking landmark on the road to post-democracy occurred during the 2000 presidential election in the US. In a very close race, there were major grounds for suspecting vote tampering had taken place in Florida, the state governed by his brother Jeb, in favour of the successful Republican candidate, George W. Bush. The issue went to the law courts. There were some demonstrations against the outcome among black Americans, but the prevailing concern in the country seemed to be that the dispute over the outcome was depressing the stock exchange, and should therefore be abandoned. In any case, only just over 50 per cent of those eligible had actually voted. In contrast, in South Africa just six years earlier, almost 87 per cent of those eligible had voted in the first general election there in which the black majority had been entitled to do so; many had queued for hours outside polling stations. That was a democratic moment.

2
Inequality and Corruption

The use of money to buy political influence is problematic for democracy. There is a tension between the equality of citizens' votes and the inequality of their economic circumstances – a major unresolved problem of liberal democracy. This tension is manageable if inequalities are modest or declining, and if economic inequality does not interfere too much with political processes. The neoliberalism that has dominated most contemporary political economy has reduced this manageability in two ways. First, it has been associated with a major increase in material inequalities; second, it has legitimated the use of wealth for political influence. The latter is, in turn, linked to a further problem: corruption.

All political and economic systems are vulnerable to corruption, but in different ways. In non-democratic systems, where governments can act in more or less complete secrecy and criticism is not allowed, corruption is routine. If one can effortlessly use the powers of the state to extract money for one's self, family and friends, why not just do it? This dynamic works whether the regime is a ruling family, as in traditional monarchies, a military dictatorship, or a state-socialist one in which a leader has amassed the resources of an all-powerful state around himself. Things are more difficult in democracies, where oppositions and prying journalists are on the lookout for anything suspicious. But much government business can be concealed from the media, and a charismatic leader with adequate parliamentary support might still be able to turn offices of state into family fiefdoms. Also, where corruption becomes endemic, opposition parties often hope to inherit the networks that nourish it when they take office and therefore avoid challenging them. Much depends on cultures of behaviour that develop within political parties and public administrations. Where corruption is more or less unheard of, it is very difficult to start it, and rules of openness and accountability will be in place to nip it in the bud. Once it becomes endemic, it can become almost impossible to root out, as so many participants have snouts at the trough.

In neoliberalism, corruption mainly takes the form of certain forms of behaviour being redefined as not corrupt. This has an affinity with post-democracy, in which public affairs are conducted by overlapping business and political elites, following rules that seem robust but which have in fact been hollowed out. We shall here consider, first, the way in which rising inequality has in itself weakened democracy, and will then go on to consider the relationship between the political use of wealth, corruption and a further weakening of democracy. (More detailed discussions of the arguments in this chapter will be found in Crouch 2015a and 2016a.)

Inequality and Democracy

Liberal democracy operates at two levels: the formal processes of elections, where rules to ensure strict equality among all citizens are usually accepted as paramount; and the informal toing and froing of debate, lobbying and pressure – everything that goes on to link the world

Inequality and Corruption

of government to the rest of society between elections. This latter is what we call 'civil society', the sphere in which social movements are active, and where the popular challenges that sustain democracy's vibrancy are located; but it is also the space within which the political power of unequal wealth is wielded. In informal politics there are no guarantees of equality. This is a dilemma of central importance to the practice of contemporary democracy.

The significance of this question depends on how economically unequal a society is. In the 1950s and 1960s, US political theorists developed the theory of pluralism, less familiarly but more accurately known as polyarchy (see Dahl 1961; 1971), to demonstrate that inequality might not be an important impediment to democracy. They argued that democracy's need for relative equality would be met if there were large numbers of groups trying to influence government, using a diversity of non-overlapping types of resource, and usually being effective only within specific, limited areas of policy. In that way, no single interest would dominate. Something like equality would be roughly achieved within the idea of 'you win some, you lose some; no one wins or loses all the time'. Democratic pluralism is analogous to the free market: provided that there are many participants in the market, all are price-takers and none can exercise significant influence by acting alone.

The pluralist model viewed the America of its day through rosy spectacles. It ignored the plight of black people in the southern states, the exaggerated anti-communist stance of Senator Joe McCarthy's activities, and the extraordinary warning given about the political power of the 'military-industrial complex' by President Eisenhower in his valedictory address in 1961. Nevertheless, the US in that period was a relatively egalitarian society, and western societies in general were experiencing probably their lowest levels of inequality in recorded history. These findings emerge from Thomas Piketty's (2013) study of long-term trends in wealth holding. But Piketty also shows that those days have passed. Since the 1980s, the period when neoliberal policies began to dominate, inequality has been rising in most developed countries, fastest of all in the US. In particular, the returns to wealth ownership have been increasing faster than those to income from work, and various mechanisms ensure that those with the very highest wealth have particularly high returns. This necessarily produces an intensification of inequalities. Increasing shares of wealth and income are going to a small minority, often reckoned to mean the top 0.1 per cent or 0.01 per cent of the income distribution.

The Organization for Economic Cooperation and Development (OECD) has identified several causes of this rise (OECD 2011: 122 ff.). Important has been the growing role of the financial sector and related business services. This has generated an extensive lobbying capacity in that sector, which probably links to another finding of the OECD study: that 'institutional' and policy factors were among the most important sources of growing inequality. Institutions and, in particular, policies are not ineluctable or neutral technical forces, but lie within the control of human decision-makers. There is therefore a mutually reinforcing process of economic and political power, a spiral whereby large increases in the wealth of the very rich enable them to influence public policy, leading to policy outcomes favouring their interests, which in turn makes them even wealthier. This can be seen particularly clearly in taxation, changes in which have been responsible for producing some of the growing inequality. Across the OECD area as a whole, the highest income tax rates declined from 66 per cent to 42 per cent between 1981 and 2010 (Förster et al.). The bottom 90 per cent of the income distribution receive between 70 per cent and 85 per cent of their income in the form of wages and salaries; the top 0.01 per cent receive only 40 per cent of their income in this form, the majority coming as corporate income, dividends and capital gains. These kinds of income have increasingly been taxed more lightly than wages and salaries. The average corporate income tax in the OECD area has declined from 47 per cent to 25 per cent between 1981 and 2010, dividend tax from 75 per cent to 42 per cent (Bastagli et al. 2012). These changes have taken place during a period when pre-tax income inequality was increasing. One might have expected that, in the face of growing pre-tax income inequality, democratically responsive fiscal regimes would improve the progressivity of taxation. Instead, in most countries, the opposite has happened, fiscal changes reinforcing the increasing inequality being produced by the market. This suggests that the interests of the rich have pressed more strongly on governments than those of democracy.

Another institutional change that the OECD identified as a cause of increasing inequality was the decline of coordinated collective bargaining. The changes directly involved here are most likely to affect inequalities within the bottom 60 per cent, as they concern the decline of solidaristic bargaining within the employed workforce. However, one can go beyond the OECD's own analysis to identify changes that affect wider inequalities and political processes. There is a close, though not perfect, relationship between the extent of coordinated collective bargaining and trade union power (measured as a combination of the density of union membership and the engagement of unions in governance mechanisms). There is also a strong correlation between trade union power and post-tax and post-transfer inequality: the greater the degree of union power, the greater the extent of redistribution produced by the fiscal system (Crouch 2016b: ch. 6). Everywhere, coordinated bargaining, union strength and fiscal redistribution have been in decline, reducing the role of what had been a major form of countervailing power against capital in more pluralist times.

A further idea of 1960s pluralism helps us understand how holders of extreme wealth can wield a power unattainable by groups of ordinary citizens. Mancur Olson (1965) developed a theory of collective action, which proposed that participation in collective political projects was very difficult to achieve. First, if a movement were big enough to be likely to succeed, it would do so without the participation of any one individual, whose contribution would be infinitesimal to the movement though costly to that individual; therefore, individuals had only a very low incentive to participate. Second, if the movement were aimed at a collective good rather than a membership good, individuals would benefit from the movement's success even if they did not participate; again, the incentive to take part was very low.

Olson's theory assumed a world in which people had no means of coordinating their actions except through voluntary individual action. This is not the situation of persons possessing considerable wealth, especially when they hold powerful positions in large corporations. They do not need members in order to establish an organization; if they want human resources, they can employ people. The coordination problem is resolved through the deployment of wealth. This was the device originally used by Silvio Berlusconi, discussed in the previous chapter. The very wealthy are therefore always an exception to the collective action problem, provided that they have enough incentive to bother to take action. They have this where governments might be in a position either to favour or to frustrate their private interests. The assumption of the old pluralist model that in a market economy firms can be seen as just some among many interests falls where giant corporations in a period of growing inequality are concerned – a circumstance that was indeed perceived and warned against by two of the leading US pluralist theorists themselves right at the start of the current period of growing inequality (Dahl 1982; Lindblom 1977).

In 2010 the International Monetary Fund (IMF) claimed that during the previous four-year electoral cycle, US firms had spent $4.2 billion on political activities, particularly prominent among them being firms in the high-risk end of the financial sector (IMF 2010). A former chief economist of the IMF, Simon Johnson, has claimed (2009) that in the years running up to the 2008 financial crisis the financial sector had captured control of US government in a manner normally associated with developing countries. The pattern has continued and grown during the presidency of Donald Trump (Potter 2018). These findings are not surprising. In the US, corporate political lobbying has been explicitly facilitated by the Supreme Court. In 2010 it rejected a ruling by the Federal Election Commission that there were limits to the sums of money that organizations could spend on election campaigns, the Court arguing that the US Constitution should be seen as having granted the same rights to organizations as to individuals. At that stage it did, however, maintain the prohibition on donations to individual candidates (US Supreme Court 2010). Four years later, however, the Court removed that ban (US Supreme Court 2014). There are now virtually no limits to the use of wealth to influence political decisions in the US.

The US is not alone in this experience. Pierre France and Antoine Vauchez (2017) have tracked the close interrelations in France between public officials and private interests. German parties receive generous state funding and therefore are not dependent on corporate money in the same way as American ones, but a recent study by the Max Planck Institute for the Study of Societies in Cologne has demonstrated how at least since the 1980s German public policies of all governing parties have followed the preferences of large corporations and wealthy elites rather than of poorer citizens (Elsässer et al. 2018). Similar studies of other western democracies would probably yield similar results. This is an important instance of how in post-democracy the core of political decision-making and favours shifts to small, overlapping political and business elites.

From lobbying to clandestine opinion manipulation

Lobbying by the very rich is mainly directed at policy-makers, using post-democracy's private circles of elites. But wealth can also be used to influence the opinions of ordinary people. The rise of social media in recent years has transformed the possibilities available. The Internet can be used to send targeted messages purporting to come from mass movements of citizens, while they are in fact being controlled by some of the richest people in the world. Billionaire or state funding is needed for these activities, as the technology involved is costly. It must first collect (often illegally) data from social media organizations on various preferences exhibited by individuals in their web searches and purchasing behaviour. Individual messages then have to be tailored to suit those preferences and are sent from a large number of apparently independent sources. It is an irony that most of this campaigning purports to come from populist challengers to elites. This considerably exceeds my vision of politics under post-democracy, as even the activities that seem to be taking place are artificial.

The first major example was the Tea Party movement founded in the US around 2009. It supports most policies associated with US conservative Republicans, including opposition to public health services, most taxation, nearly all business regulation and all action to combat pollution and arrest climate change. It styles itself a grassroots movement, and gives the impression of relying on resources pouring into its organization from large numbers of individuals, who also shape its agenda; in reality, it is heavily funded by a small number of billionaires, mainly the Koch brothers, who control its policies. This has led the Tea Party's wittier critics to style it an 'Astroturf' movement. It is an example of how the very rich do not confront the logic of collective action that limits the capacity of ordinary citizens to organize movements. The Koch brothers and other major wealth-holders also fund a wide range of academic research institutes and think-tanks in the US, the UK and elsewhere that support anti-regulation causes, giving the impression that a diversity of voices is urging similar solutions (see Diamond 1995 for an early study of this phenomenon). More recently, Nancy MacLean (2018) studied the role of billionaire funding in spreading the influence of neoliberal public choice theory in US universities and think-tanks.

Jamie Susskind (2018) has analysed the transfer of power that takes place when, in using the Internet, we (usually unconsciously) allow masses of information about ourselves to pass to those who have the wealth and the motive to run the technologies that can accumulate and use such data to aim messages at us. Much of this is used by corporations to target commercial advertising towards individuals, but, as Susskind shows, it has major political implications. People are more likely to believe that an event has taken place, or that a view is sound, if it seems to come to their personal social media site from many different points than if it comes from just one. Disguising single-source messages as multiple ones therefore conveys considerable political power. Social media, which seemed at one point to offer a new commons, a public space open to all comers, have in fact led to a privatization of civil society itself, as its spaces become owned by the super-rich.

Thanks to research carried out by a British investigative journalist, Carole Cadwalladr, attention has focused in particular on the role of a US billionaire, Robert Mercer, who, through various channels, funded Cambridge Analytica, a technology firm that specialized in this kind of centralized message crowding. Mercer is close to Donald Trump, and Cambridge Analytica was active in both Trump's presidential election campaign in 2016 and in illegally supporting the successful campaign to have the UK leave the EU in the same year. There is also strong, officially endorsed evidence that the Russian government played a role in cyber-activity in the Brexit campaign and the Trump elections, illegally channelling around £8 million into the pro-Brexit movement (UK Electoral

Commission 2018). The Oxford Internet Institute has calculated that during 2017 there were political campaigns of financially organized social media manipulation in 48 countries (Howard and Woolley 2018).

As with this last example, the main use of this kind of messaging has been to support xenophobic and other forms of socially conservative populist movements. These have a paradoxical relationship to neoliberalism, the role of wealth and post-democracy, and we shall return to consider them in greater detail in Chapter 5. For present purposes, the relevant link is that between inequalities of wealth and a capacity to organize a highly post-democratic form of illusory civil society action.

Redefining Corruption

Other neoliberal challenges to democracy can best be considered under the heading of corruption. In theory, political corruption should not occur in neoliberal capitalist economic regimes. According to classical economic theory, in a pure market economy, government should play only a minor role, so there is little to gain from trying to buy influence over it. The role of government should be limited to maintaining strong competition within the market by preventing monopoly and oligopoly. Corruption should occur only in regimes where the state works hand in glove with favoured firms or what in France used to be known as 'national champions'. Also, in the best classic liberal public service traditions of the nineteenth to the mid-twentieth centuries there were strict rules to ensure an arm's-length relationship between public officials and private firms, mirroring the relationship that was supposed to exist between politics and the economy in the market economy. These rules, although economically liberal in origin, were also highly congenial to social democratic parties, which were suspicious of the influence of wealthy business interests. There was therefore a widespread consensus over such rules, even if in practice corruption and the illegitimate influence of wealth over policies often occurred.

Surprisingly, given that we usually associate neoliberalism with neoclassical economics, neoliberals have broken with these traditions, using two separate arguments: a changed approach to the meaning of competition; and the adoption of New Public Management (NPM). For some neoliberal thinkers, competition offering consumers actual choice is less important than efficiency that improves 'consumer welfare'. Followers of NPM are also less concerned with a need to separate economy and polity than with a belief that the state and public sector are highly incompetent. Therefore, while they persist with the view that the state should not interfere with business, they take the opposite view of the intervention of business in the state, which is seen as very likely to improve the performance of the latter. They are also hostile to the idea of public services, but consider that if they must exist they should be delivered by private firms. This leads to a third change in classical approaches to the public/private division. All three developments carry high risks of corruption and contribute further to the creation of post-democratic business and political elites remote from ordinary citizens. We shall consider them in turn.

Imperfect competition and corporate neoliberalism

Neoclassical economic theory depends on a vision of the market as a place where masses of producers and consumers come together. In such a situation the concept of power is abolished, which is why the idea of the pure market runs alongside that of formal democracy, defining a world of relatively low inequality and pluralism. In a pure market, it is easy for new participants to enter and for the inefficient to leave. The existence of a large mass of producers does not just guarantee choice for consumers, but also means that no one or small group of producers can exercise domination. There is certainly inequality of returns, since the pursuit of wealth is the incentive that the system provides to producers to improve and to innovate in order to attract customers. But inequality will be limited, since the emergence of high incomes in a particular activity or sector serves as a signal to others to enter it, increasing supply so that earnings decline. This will happen if the condition of ease of entry for new producers is fulfilled.

So important are these conditions that classic economic theory, however resistant to an economic role for the state in many respects, insists on strong competition authorities, which will break up monopolies or situations where there are two few producers to sustain true markets. However, in some important sectors of the economy it is very difficult to maintain large numbers of firms. Some (such as energy, mass motor vehicle, aircraft and shipping production, or bulk pharmaceuticals) require very large investments, which act as major barriers to entry for new producers. Others, such as mass-production foods, require large distribution networks, with similar effects. Very recently we have witnessed the rapid emergence of vast monopoly corporations in the information technology (IT) sector. At first, the growth of the Internet provided opportunities for a large number of new entrepreneurial firms. In some areas this is still the case, but, as its name implies, the Internet is a set of networks, and networks have an important economic characteristic. The value of a network depends on its size, with particular advantages flowing to the largest of all. No one wants to choose the tenth largest of a group of available networks. The technical term that economists use for this process is 'network externality'. A very small number of monopolistic Internet-based firms has therefore rapidly emerged, and these corporations (e.g., Apple, Microsoft, Google, Facebook) have almost overnight become the largest firms in the world. There is then a secondary development of platform firms, corporations that use the Internet to market services that are not in themselves part of the IT sector itself: taxi services, parcel and food delivery, short-stay hotel bookings and, in the case of Amazon, a wide range of both services and products. These share the same logic of networks: a user of a platform normally wants the biggest possible one. There is a further factor: where monopoly (or at least highly restricted competition) is a feasible goal, corporations can afford to run at a loss for several years, laying down their networks and pricing so low that they drive out smaller competitors, until the prize of network dominance is gained and prices can move upwards.

Economists have divided into those who accept no other solution to the problem than to keep working at establishing perfect competition, and those who argue that advantages flow from imperfect competition, and that therefore attempts to establish a perfectly competitive economy should be abandoned (Bork 1993 [1978]; Posner 2001). These latter try to demonstrate that returns to scale are more or less infinite, and that therefore there are no reasons on grounds of 'consumer welfare' – a concept that they elevate above 'consumer choice' – to seek to establish perfect markets. For them, unlike pure neoclassical theorists, a competitive order exists when some firms have won the competition and thereafter dominate, not when competition is permanent. We can here draw a distinction between two types of neoliberalism: between market neoliberals, whose main concern is that markets function, and corporate neoliberals, who mainly defend the role of large, oligopolistic corporations. This division is not just a matter of theory, but of practical competition law. Market neoliberals have clung to what is known in US law as 'anti-trust', seeking to break down corporate concentrations, while commercial courts sympathetic to corporate neoliberal arguments have taken a more lenient approach.

Corporate neoliberals rarely confront the political implications of increased inequality and the accumulation of wealth that could be used for political purposes to which their approach leads, but if they do it is to argue that, if governments abstained from interference in the economy, there would be nothing to lobby about and firms would have no incentive to be politically active. This argument is *faux naïf*, and not only because of the dependence of capitalist economies on government support for risk-bearing innovation and important infrastructure. As was demonstrated in the financial crisis and will be discussed in detail in the following chapter, certain sectors can be both dominated by a small number of firms and so strategically important for a national (or the global) economy that the collapse of a small number of them could provoke a massive shock to the whole system. This is the 'too big to fail' argument. It is clearly the case for banking; it is probably also true for energy, defence and (to anticipate an argument developed in more detail below) for certain privatized public services. Although both market neoliberal and social democratic critics argue that a number of large corporations need to be allowed to fail, to avoid moral hazard among the survivors on future occasions, it is difficult in practice for governments to remain indifferent to the fate of certain sectors. It is not possible to specify the full list of activities that have these characteristics; persuading governments that a particular industry has them is part of the lobbying process through which firms try to exercise political influence. Firms in such sectors then have a clear incentive to become politicized, as they have much to gain from government, even if government itself would prefer not to become involved. There is also evidence from Germany that, the more concentrated that ownership is within a particular sector, the higher the share of income that goes to capital, and the lower to labour, reinforcing overall trends to increased inequality (Ponattu et al. 2018). The uneven distribution of political influence that all this implies among businesses in different sectors, let alone in comparison with the rest of the population, embodies part of the asymmetry and inequality that makes the whole process of business lobbying questionable on both market-economic and democratic grounds.

Inequality and Corruption

Neoliberal thinkers like to depict the potentially corrupting relationships between governments and favoured corporations as something typical of Japanese or Korean 'crony capitalism', or the former statist capitalism of France and Italy, features that would be swept clean by neoliberal reforms. Nothing of the kind has happened. Instead, neoliberalism has merely provided a new legitimation for light or non-existent regulation that permits such relationships to persist. This reality was dramatically illustrated in early 2019 when 356 people were killed in two air crashes, affecting Indonesian and Ethiopian airlines, and both involving a Boeing 737 Max 8 airliner. Boeing is a flagship company for the US, engaged in global competition with the EU's Airbus. In order to get a sophisticated new plane quickly into service, it is alleged that Boeing had cut corners over design and testing. Although the US has an independent Federal Aviation Authority (FAA), its budget and powers have been cut in successive waves of neoliberal 'reform', to the extent that it permits Boeing itself to carry out the safety tests that are the responsibility of the FAA. It seems that the tests were inadequate: a basic fault went undiscovered; the plane went into service; 356 people died.

The contemporary economy is one in which monopolistic and anti-competitive tendencies are very strong. Although we should not write off the capacity of competition authorities – and especially the European Court of Justice (ECJ) – to tackle the issue, these authorities are themselves an example of how impossible it is to disentangle polity and economy. Where market competition cannot ensure quality and safety, only regulation can help us; but neoliberal policies reduce the strength of regulation, and wealthy corporations can find means of capturing or undermining regulatory activities. The doctrine that business involvement in government was positive and only government involvement in business was negative therefore appeared at a particularly unfortunate time, and has contributed heavily to post-democracy by reinforcing the temptation of the political class to cluster thickly around business elites.

New public management

Neoliberal thinking became critical of classic liberal ideas concerning the distance that should govern relations between public officials and business people. It argued that these had led to public services becoming cut off from developments in the private sector, where competitive pressures led to constant innovation in ways of working. Former ideas were displaced by NPM theory, the aim of which is to enable government and public services to become more like the private sector. This has encouraged the development of close relationships between politicians and public officials on the one side and firms with whom they do business on the other, on the grounds that this would enable private business thinking to percolate into government. The barrier between polity and economy became a semi-permeable membrane: firms should interfere with government, but not vice versa. This has become a major mechanism for legitimating what used to be seen as corrupt practice and for intensifying the threat posed to democracy by growing inequality.

Taken together, monopoly tendencies and NPM have greatly facilitated political lobbying by business interests. An important example has been the International Life Sciences Institute, an organization that has claimed to be a neutral scientific organization, formally advising the EU and the US government on food health issues. Research has shown that it appears to be a lobby for corporations in the food industry, seeking to undermine research on the harmful effects of sugars and other food industry products (Steele et al. 2019).

Private sector consultants have seeped deeply into government circles, not only offering advice but designing policies, even being able to recommend their own products for purchase by public authorities. This has, for example, often happened with recommendations for government acquisition of computer systems. Staff members from US health firms were appointed to advisory posts in the UK Department of Health in order to assist in the construction of a role for private firms in health provision. Politicians and civil servants leaving public office have been permitted to work as consultants to private firms, using their former government contacts to help the firms win public contracts. Technology advisors to the administrations of both Barak Obama and Donald Trump have been able to move on to senior executive positions with Amazon, using their contacts to facilitate the purchase of Amazon technology by US government departments. It has become routine for British ministers of various parties to enter business relationships with firms in sectors for which they had responsibilities when leaving office. On leaving office, the social democratic chancellor of Germany Gerhard Schröder, who oversaw major contracts for the supply of Russian gas to the country, joined the board of Gazprom, the Russian energy giant. This 'revolving door' behaviour was contrary to all rules under earlier systems of public/private relations. It certainly occurred, but it was vulnerable to criticism and sanction; today it is boasted about. Discovering these connections does not therefore require extensive research. Whether or not actual corruption is involved is probably beside the point; corruption is unnecessary when interlocking interests of this kind can operate brazenly.

A major example was the subcontracting of many military and oil exploitation activities to private firms by the US administration of George W. Bush in its wars in Afghanistan and Iraq. Partly because of claims to a need for secrecy in such a context, many of these large contracts were awarded without a competitive bidding process. Prominent among the firms involved was Halliburton, of which the vice-president of the US, Richard Cheney, a major advocate of these wars, had previously been chairman and CEO. Another example was the extraordinary lobbying campaign unleashed by the US health industry against the Obama administration's healthcare reform policy. It was reported (by the UK's *Guardian* newspaper on 1 October 2009) that US health insurance firms, hospitals and pharmaceutical corporations deployed six lobbyists for each member of Congress and spent $380 million campaigning against the policy. 'Campaigning' primarily meant contributing to the re-election funds of sitting congresspersons. Although the legislation was eventually passed, it was diluted in many important ways, ensuring, in particular, that the scheme that finally passed provided compulsory, partly subsidized customers for private corporations.

The outsourcing of public services

A major new field for a growing political power of private capital has opened with the privatization and outsourcing of public services. Transferring public services away from direct management by public bodies to the market is commended by NPM as bringing advantages of efficiency, stronger control over how professionals do their work, and greater choice for users. This assumes that, with outsourcing, these professions come under a true market regime of a wide number and diversity of providers. In practice this rarely happens. In a 2012 study of how the new market in childcare is developing in the UK, Social Enterprise UK (a body representing social enterprise organizations) complained that small providers were being squeezed out of the field by private equity corporations, whose business model enables them to compete much more successfully for contracts to run children's homes. 'Social enterprise' is a form of business that conforms to NPM, as it involves allowing competing nonstate providers to enter the delivery of social services and applying some commercial practices to activities that previously belonged to the state and public service professionals. But it is not structured for pure profit maximization, and social enterprise firms find it very difficult to compete with standard shareholder businesses.

A small number of corporations dominate outsourcing markets in the UK, and the British state has become dependent on them. It is notable that these firms win contracts across an extraordinarily wide range of activities, from military support to the provision of social care, fields where they had no prior expertise in the particular bodies of professional knowledge involved or past track record. Their core business is not a particular field of activity in which they have expertise, but knowing how to win government contracts: which often means how to develop contacts with officials and politicians. Evoking the phrase used about the giant banks that had to be rescued during the financial crisis, Social Enterprise (2012) commented that these private contractors had become 'too big to fail', so central had they become to providing Britain's public services and infrastructure. Indeed, they have been occasionally fined for abuses in their performance of these roles, and have handed contracts back; but they keep being awarded new ones. Others have undergone major financial crises because of the ways in which they used their secure public contracting role to acquire an unsustainable ranking on stock exchanges. Major examples have included Carillion, a giant construction and general contracting firm that collapsed with £2 billion of debts in 2018, and Interserve, a contractor providing a wide range of public services from school meals to offender rehabilitation, which collapsed later in the same year. The government had tried to save such firms by awarding them even more contracts, with subsequent costs to taxpayers. Either these corporations have become so big that government is dependent on them, or their hold on the contract-winning system has become impregnable.

Outsourcing services is usually presented as removing a service from state monopoly into the realm of customer choice. However, outsourcing contracts are awarded by public authorities. These are therefore the customers;

the general public are simply users, pseudo-customers. The contractors' responsibility is to the public authority, whose interests are not necessarily identical to those of users. Further, by their nature many of these contracts have to run for long periods of time, sometimes for more than 20 years; one cannot frequently renegotiate contracts to run schools or hospitals. Therefore the market exists only at very separated, discrete points of time when contracts are up for tender. In outsourced public service provision, we are confronted by a distinctive organizational form: a licensed private monopoly, a business model usually associated with medieval economies. Meanwhile, as public authorities contract out services, they lose any expertise or knowledge that is needed to run them, and are, as a result, unable to evaluate the competence and performance of the firms that have taken over the contract. In addition to being likely to lead to inferior service, this further increases the dependence of government on a small number of firms in the private sector, as only they will possess the professional knowledge required. These activities are too political and oligopolistic to be part of the true market economy, while democracy seems unable to penetrate the networks that sustain them. For some years it has been clear that, whatever the failings of publicly provided services have sometimes been, there are no systematic, guaranteed advantages of private provision.

Conclusion

Growing inequality and large concentrations of wealth in businesses that are too big to fail are distorting and rendering highly undemocratic the informal politics of lobbying and pressure that democracy itself needs. Under the guise of an ideology, neoliberalism, which claims to assert the importance of barriers between public and private power, we are witnessing a new fusion of the two, under the dominance of various privileged corporate interests. We are forced to ask, alongside such recent observers as Wolfgang Merkel (2014), and Wolfgang Streeck (2015a) whether capitalism and democracy are today as mutually reinforcing as they once seemed to be, or indeed even mutually compatible. Capitalist businesspeople are usually believed to have a preference for democracy because they tend not to like dictatorships, which use heavy state power, can be arbitrary and change rules without due process. Current enthusiasm for investment in China casts some doubt on that generalization, but it is the case that the Pinochet regime in Chile remains highly unusual for having been a cruel and ruthless regime that nevertheless maintained the non-interventionist, strict neoliberal economic strategy prepared by its Chicago-trained advisors. Modern democracy more or less guarantees the rule of law, and clear procedures for changing law and lobbying around proposed changes. On the other hand, democracy can produce a mass of regulations to protect non-market, non-corporate interests. Capitalists' preferred regime is post-democracy, where all the forms of democracy continue, including importantly the rule of law, but where the electorate has become passive, not engaging in disturbing activism, and not generating a civil society vibrant enough to produce awkward counter-lobbies that try to rival the quiet work of business interests in the corridors of government.

Post-democratic capitalism does not require a formal renunciation of democracy any more than corporate neoliberalism requires a renunciation of the market; indeed, democracy and the market continue to be used together as the primary legitimation of the evolving political system of dominant corporate power, because this latter lacks any legitimation of its own. Elements for such a legitimation are there, but they are used in a supplementary way (Crouch 2015b). Corporate neoliberals have provided a justification for protecting market-dominating corporations from market-making competition law. NPM theory legitimates the abolition of boundaries between public officials and corporate personnel seen so important to an earlier age of liberal economy. Going beyond themes we have discussed here, corporate social responsibility both gives business leaders a social legitimation going beyond their role as profit-maximizers and suggests that public policy is not needed to tackle many market failures. In the absence of Keynesian demand management, the widespread desire for a high level of employment gives priority to the policy preferences of business interests.

We have not yet arrived at a situation where corporate dominance of our politics is complete; otherwise, all consumer protection and labour laws would have already been abolished. But this is the direction of travel, strengthened by continuing growth in inequality and the mutual reinforcement of political and economic power.

3
The 2008 Financial Crisis

In his masterly study of the 2008 financial crisis, Adam Tooze (2018) records how, just a year before, Alan Greenspan, the recently retired chair of the US Federal Reserve who had presided over much of the financial deregulation programme in the US, said in answer to a question about voting in the forthcoming US presidential election: '[We] are fortunate that, thanks to globalization, policy decisions in the US have been largely replaced by global market forces. National security aside, it hardly makes any difference who will be the next president. The world is governed by market forces.' Assuming that Greenspan did not believe that elections, though more or less pointless, should be abolished, this is a rare example of overt advocacy of post-democracy.

The crisis itself brought striking confirmation of the importance of interlocking political and business elites and their subversion of democracy in two different ways: first, in the process of lobbying that preceded it; and second in the way in which banking interests were prioritized in the wake of the crisis. The case also richly demonstrated the irony of neoliberalism: that its proclaimed virtues of the separation of economy and polity and the importance of transparency were completely transgressed in its flagship project, the deregulation of financial services. We shall first set out the main issues involved in the political background to the crisis, and then ask whether it was an instance of post-democracy. Finally, putting the question differently – would stronger democracy have prevented the crisis? – suggests some disturbing answers.

How Financial Markets Were Deregulated

Following the financial crash and subsequent prolonged depression starting in 1929, the US and some other governments established clear rules to reduce the impact that irresponsible behaviour in the banking system could have on the rest of the economy and society. Banks were permitted to borrow to fund investments only up to a certain ratio of their actual assets. This was designed to ensure that, if some of their investments failed, the damage inflicted on others by their inability to repay debts would be limited. Further, investment bank activities had to be separated from general banking. This would ensure that banks did not use the assets of ordinary customers to fund speculative and risky activities. Also stemming from that period came a number of rules to ensure general honesty in corporate accounting. Companies were required to have their accounts audited by entirely independent accountants. Later, in the reconstruction of the world system that followed the Second World War, the governments of the western world, meeting at Bretton Woods in New Hampshire, agreed a system of financial governance. The values of currencies were fixed in relation to the US dollar, with changes in these values being political decisions by governments, not the results of currency market speculation; and governments exercised controls over movements of capital. This approach reinforced the stability of the financial system initiated in the 1930s.

Matters began to unravel in 1972, when the US pulled out of the Bretton Woods arrangement. Currency speculation and the establishment of private markets in currencies produced a highly unstable regime. Tooze shows how the roots of the dominance of giant banks over the financial system date from that time. From then on, political choices to reduce regulation produced an eventually dangerously uncontrollable system. Starting in the 1980s, most of the banking rules established in the 1930s were gradually relaxed, in the name of neoliberal reform. This initially affected the US and UK economies, but later spread to much of the rest of the world. The argument was that deregulation would remove the chains from enterprise and grow the economy. If banks could take more risks, they would be able to create more wealth.

Changes also took place in corporate governance. Again following American and British examples, either company law or just company practice in many economies was reformed to establish the maximization of shareholder value (i.e., the share price) as the sole goal of a company. (For some critical evaluations of this process, see Driver and Thompson 2018.) Really smart investors can arrange their finances so that they win whatever actually happens to firms and their profits. As Helen Callaghan (2018) has explained in a study of the process as it affected Britain, France and Germany, all that matters to them is that shareholder interests dominate corporate governance, and they have successfully lobbied governments to ensure that this takes place. Michel Feher (2018) has further shown that profit from actual business activity is no longer the goal of companies; it has been replaced by short-term share price. Known as 'mark to market', this became the standard means by which accountants and auditors assessed the value of an enterprise. These developments have fundamentally changed the original idea of classical economic theory that profit is a residual, what is left of a firm's earnings after suppliers, employees and other claimants on its resources have been paid. In contemporary markets, if share values drop below expectations, firms face takeover bids from groups who believe that they can manage the firm in a way that will deliver a higher share price. Senior executives must deliver a certain level of appreciation in share value or face very severe consequences.

Shareholders' expected earnings have replaced profit, and are not a residual but have to reach guaranteed levels, and over very short time horizons. Achieving these targets has become de facto the *first* charge on a firm, before consideration is given to pricing, research and development, or employee interests. Shareholders cease to be the primary risk-bearers. One of the key objectives of this turn in corporate governance was to ensure that senior managers followed shareholders' interests. Linking their own remuneration to share price levels was seen as key to this, though there is considerable evidence that the pay of senior executives in large corporations continues to rise even when share values decline (Reiff 2013: ch. 4). The principal incentive of senior executives is to produce a climate in which potential and existing shareholders believe that the firm will have successful activities. Devoting resources to research and development or other activities might reduce short-term share appreciation and therefore hinder a firm's stock market performance. Meanwhile, new digitalized stock markets have enabled shares to be traded at high velocity, sometimes being owned for fractions of a second before computer algorithms signal that it would be profitable to sell. At the very moment when shareholders' interests in a firm have become the only ones recognized, shareholders themselves are ceasing to be owners in any meaningful sense of the word.

Taken together, the deregulation measures and the elevation of share prices have given priority in the financial sector to secondary markets – that is, markets in which people buy and sell stocks and shares in a firm in the expectation of selling them on rather than to profit from trading activities in its actual products. Purchasers of these assets base their assessments of value on what they in turn think they can sell them for, and so on almost *ad infinitum*. All valuations of companies have become based on what others believe others will believe (and so on), with the funds used to buy the assets at each stage being in turn based on what bank lenders believed the assets might one day be worth. It is this process that accounts for the fact that firms in highly fashionable sectors (particularly the Internet) have had stock exchange valuations of vast worth before they have sold a single product. In a further deregulatory measure, banks were allowed to fund investments way above their own asset levels. This enabled them to venture ever larger sums in the secondary markets, intensifying the spiralling rise in asset prices. They were still taking risks, but at each stage a given investor would sell on shares to a larger number of further investors, each person's (or firm's) risk being reduced by being shared with larger numbers. As the system expanded and wealthy people in China, Russia and several other parts of the world previously outside the capitalist market system joined the game, more and more investors were sharing the risks. There seemed to be an almost infinite expansion of risk sharing, and therefore of risk reduction. Wealth was being created, not out of the production of actual goods and services, but out of the successive upward repricing of financial assets as they were repetitively bought and resold.

Financial activities became by far the most profitable forms of economic activity: making money just by dealing in money, cutting out the middle activities of making goods or providing services that are sold for profit. For firms in other sectors of the economy this presented a strong incentive, first to acquire a financial arm and then to concentrate expertise and strategic effort in that arm, with other activities, including original core business functions and mass customer relations, being contracted out in various ways (Fligstein and Shin 2007; van der Zwan 2014). Modern economies have thus become rooted in financial transactions based on expectations and the sharing of risk.

The deregulation of international capital movements gave finance a freedom and flexibility not enjoyed by labour and other factors of production. Finance capital is highly mobile, while states, working populations and firms with committed plant and equipment remain grounded in their territories. The party to an arrangement that can most easily defect and go elsewhere usually has the upper hand. This has increasingly become the case for finance capital. As ever more assets of the largest firms were converted into financial ones, the proportion of capital that enjoyed this mobility grew. Governments in most countries were eager to attract this free-floating capital, adopted 'mark to market' forms of corporate governance that favoured its interests, and became generally willing to modify social, labour and environmental policies to attract it. Governments could of course have combined together to defend their interests against mobile capital – and to a greater extent than elsewhere countries in the EU have been willing to do that – but they have usually fallen for the temptation to play 'beggar my neighbour', offering ever lower corporate taxes and deregulated environments in order to lure free-floating capital away from others.

Economics, traditionally known as the 'dismal science', because it talked about scarcity and the need to make choices, became the science that told us we could have it all. Although the main activities of the deregulated financial system primarily concerned, and massively rewarded, operators in the financial markets themselves, crumbs fell from rich men's tables into the laps of ordinary people. Because risks could be repeatedly resold and shared, it became easier for nearly everyone to get loans on soft terms, in particular home buyers, primarily in the US but also in the UK, Ireland, Spain and a few other economies with easy-going mortgage systems. Not only could mortgages be found by people with virtually no security beyond the mortgage itself, but homes could be re-mortgaged in order to fund consumption, expanding further the amount of credit in the system that was not backed by anything other than the belief that the system could go on expanding.

In retrospect, the extreme instability of all these arrangements seems clear, and a few brave individuals pointed it out at the time, but they were ignored. The financial markets, which now accounted for a large proportion of global wealth, were based on beliefs about beliefs about beliefs (and so on) of what other investors believed assets were worth. Operators felt no need to enquire into what actual risks were involved in buying and reselling a mass of mortgage debts at several times the primary market value of the properties involved. The system of independent corporate audit provided few correctives to the process, partly because auditors themselves adopted 'mark-to-market' rules, and partly because further deregulation moves permitted audit firms also to earn large sums from management consultancy contracts with their audit clients, reducing their independence of the client. Furthermore, although any one risk could be widely shared and therefore any individual investor's part in it became minute, the sheer quantity of high-risk loans being traded meant that an individual investor might well hold a large accumulation of, albeit minute, shares at any one time.

The financial markets were becoming a game of pass the parcel, in which the parcel contained a bomb that would explode as soon as the parcel stopped moving. It was important to ensure not just that the parcel was not in one's own hands when the music stopped, but that the music would never stop, since, if the bomb went off, everyone would be damaged. While the parcel was circulating, no one had an incentive to enquire what was in it; time would be better spent passing it on.

The first signs of the inherent fragility of the system came in 1998 with the collapse of Long-Term Capital Management (LTCM). This was a hedge fund management firm, founded only four years earlier, based on a mathematical algorithm that balanced investments in safe and high-risk securities in a manner that seemed to guarantee high returns. Hedge funds pool the resources of the extremely wealthy people who manage them. Because the initial risks are born by these individuals, the sector is hardly regulated at all. By 1998, LTCM had $5 billion of equity, but because of the confidence with which other financial institutions regarded its algorithm, it was able to leverage loans of $125 billion. During that year, an existing East Asian debt crisis was followed by a collapse of the Russian economy. Risk spreads were moving in the opposite direction from the expectations of LTCM's algorithm, and it reported its possible imminent collapse to the Federal Reserve Bank of New York. The Fed feared that the knock-on effects from such a collapse could threaten a systemic collapse, and organized a rescue by the LTCM's leading creditors. The rescue was successful, but LTCM was liquidated a year later. During the investigation into what had gone wrong, it became clear that the banks lending money to LTCM had hardly enquired at all into the nature of the fund's investments, and the fund itself had been far from transparent. In a study of the crisis published a year later, Franklin Edwards (1999) pointed to the need for regulatory action to prevent systemic crises being caused in this way. With Frederic Mishkin, Edwards had already warned in 1995 of the inherent instability of the growth of high-risk investment activities by the banking sector (Edwards and Mishkin 1995). These warnings were ignored amidst the deregulatory fervour.

Two years after the LTCM collapse came the dot-com crisis. This was the period of the initial growth of the Internet economy. Many investors had little substantive knowledge of this new sector, but since there was a general belief that it represented the future, the shares of firms within it could be sold on to others that shared that belief. Some firms found that merely adding 'dot-com' to their names could, overnight, massively increase their stock exchange valuation. It was not necessary for them to have any successful products. This increase in value could then be used to fund further speculations and to reward senior executives. This was a classic investment bubble; it started in 1995 and in 2000 it burst, causing widespread disruption to share prices and leading to many bankruptcies. The most significant of these was that of WorldCom, a telecommunications company whose collapse in 2002 resulted in the largest ever US bankruptcy by that time.

The WorldCom case also helped laid bare the risk of corrupt auditing produced by financial deregulation that had first been revealed following the collapse the previous year of the energy company Enron. At the time of its demise, Enron was the seventh largest corporation in the US and a major donor to the 2000 presidential election campaign of George W. Bush. Until overtaken by WorldCom a year later, Enron's $64 billion bankruptcy was the largest in US history. In both cases the auditors had been Arthur Andersen, a leading global firm of accountants, which in turn then disappeared from the market when its conduct in the WorldCom and Enron cases was revealed. Corporate lobbying provided the background to these scandals. Lobbyists had persuaded the US Congress to pass legislation allowing an accountancy firm employed by a corporation to be the 'independent' auditor of its accounts also to sell it other consultancy services. This had previously been illegal because of the incentive it might give audit firms to keep quiet about irregularities they found in corporate accounts. This is precisely what happened, quite soon after the legislation was passed. Enron had major irregularities in its accounts; Arthur Andersen audited them, and the irregularities were found, but senior management hushed them up because of the important consultancy contracts they had with Enron. Very similar events were revealed in the case of WorldCom. It is to the credit of US pluralism that the scandal could not be kept secret. The matter went to the courts and several senior executives found themselves in prison. (For a detailed analysis of the case, see Froud et al. 2004.)

One of the advantages of a capitalist economy is that, if markets are working properly, the fate of no one firm can have system-wide effects. This proved to be the case with Enron, WorldCom and Arthur Andersen. Some directors went to prison; firms disappeared; their assets were acquired by others; the gaps were filled; the markets moved on. However, these cases contained some more general, systemic lessons that were ignored. The absence of diligent scrutiny by investors revealed by the LTCM case, the dot-com crisis and the corporate scandals should all have alerted those active in financial markets to the danger that doubts would eventually be cast on the massive unexamined transactions taking place throughout those markets. Since virtually every major and minor bank had been participating in them, with truly vast sums of unsecured debt being traded, there was now a high risk that systemic damage was looming. Following the Arthur Andersen scandal, there was renewed legislation in the US to bar accountants from taking on other contracts with firms for which they acted as auditors. Otherwise, the potentially unmanageable risks in financial markets were ignored by both those active in the markets and the public agencies intended to oversee their activities. Bankers and other investors were doing extremely well out of the system, and the general public was also benefiting from the apparent growth in wealth, leading politicians and public agencies to avoid asking questions. And most, though not all, experts were advising that the model was virtually foolproof.

In August 2005 an event was held in Wyoming to celebrate the retirement of Greenspan, who had presided over most of the deregulation of the US banking sector. One speaker at the event, the IMF's chief economist, Raghuram Rajan, warned that excessive risks were being taken with financial products so complex that hardly anyone understood them, and that the danger of a banking collapse was real (Chakrabortty 2018). He was ridiculed by other participants. In the same year, the OECD expressed concern over the extent of debts being undertaken by relatively low-income households in several countries. Holders of large household debts are usually wealthy, engaged in investment projects backed by high security. The new phenomenon was unsecured debt among households that would stand little chance of repaying in the event of a financial crisis that devalued their assets. No public authority saw the warning signal that the report contained.

In 2007, there were concerns about the viability of Northern Rock, a British bank that had, until 1997, been a building society. Building societies are highly regulated financial organizations that specialize in mortgage lending to medium-income families for the purchase of residential property. They have the legal status of 'mutuals', being owned not by shareholders, but by large numbers of small savers who become voting members of the society. There are no shares to trade and their ability to borrow in order to invest outside this framework is very limited. Since the early 1990s, successive UK governments had encouraged building societies to convert themselves into banks, so that they could join in the deregulated financial system of highly leveraged loans and shareholder value maximization. The law was changed so that current building society members could, in consideration for a one-off financial reward, vote to give up their rights as mutual owners. Many building societies, though by no means all, took this step, among them Northern Rock. As a building society, it specialized in housing loans to families in one of the poorest regions of the UK, and was therefore particularly vulnerable to the risks attached to unsecured loans. Liberated from building society constraints, Northern Rock rapidly became one of the biggest banks in the UK. When general doubts started to be expressed about the risks of unsecured housing loans – what in the US are known as 'sub-prime' mortgages – investors rapidly began to withdraw from Northern Rock. The panic spread to ordinary savers, who started removing their money. Within days, the bank collapsed, and the government intervened to acquire its assets.

The damage to Northern Rock investors was limited, but doubts had now been cast over the viability of the role of sub-prime mortgages in the financial system as a whole. A growing number of investment houses discovered that a high proportion of their assets were constituted by such loans, and they began to withdraw their money. The next to face crisis was Lehman Brothers, the fourth largest US investment bank. It was allowed to go bankrupt, overtaking WorldCom's record as the largest US bankruptcy. There was now a serious prospect of a general banking collapse, with knock-on effects elsewhere. The situation seemed similar to the 1930s, the Wall Street collapse that had triggered the extensive regulatory system that had gradually been demolished since the 1980s. Governments across the world acted quickly in a concerted action led by Gordon Brown, the then British prime minister. Banks were either temporarily nationalized, or at least had their assets secured by government undertakings. In 1931, countries had acted to save themselves, abjuring collective action; the consequence had been a major economic disaster, leading to massive unemployment, and contributing to the rise of nationalism that characterized the 1930s, most prominently the coming to power in Germany of Adolf Hitler and the Second World War. The response in 2008 was superior to 1931, in that there was international cooperation.

Although the system had been 'saved', the costs and negative consequences were severe for almost everyone outside the financial sector itself. Many trillions of dollars of public money were spent across the world on bailing out the banks. Eventually, part of this was repaid, as banks were resold to the private sector, but in the meantime, since ruling neoliberal ideas hold that public debt is, in principle, bad, arrangements had to be made for repaying these public debts as quickly as possible. This was usually interpreted to mean reductions in public spending programmes, including health, education, social care, police services and public administration. The reduction in public spending

The 2008 Financial Crisis

implied a general reduction in demand, and therefore increases in business failures, unemployment and poverty. Especially in the US, the homes of many low-income families with unsecured mortgages were repossessed by their lenders, rendering them homeless and reduced to living in caravans. Among members of the single European currency with high public debt, a further crisis broke in 2010 as they were placed under exceptional stress to repay their debts in order to avoid damaging the status of the euro itself. The actions surrounding this will be discussed separately in Chapter 4, as they raise their own issues of democracy.

The main outcome of the 2008 crisis was therefore a reduction in the living standards of the great majority of people, and a consequent growth in feelings of insecurity. Employment levels were gradually restored, but frequently with inferior and insecure forms of contract. Public services nearly everywhere suffered long-term damage. Living standards took a major step backwards; for the first time in many years, populations were unable to look forward to gradually growing incomes year on year. To some extent at least, this was inevitable. Much of the increase in incomes since the 1990s had been an illusion, based on the growth of financial asset prices in the secondary markets that did not represent substantive growth. A serious correction was inevitable, though there was room for debate over how that correction should be distributed across the population, between public and private sectors and over time. In most countries the main burden was born by lower and lower-middle earners. The very poorest were spared some of the impact through social policy, but after a year or two of adjustment the richest escaped largely unscathed.

The banks, whose behaviour had caused the problems in the first place, seemed relatively immune from the damage. It was generally accepted by governments and international agencies that confidence would not be restored to the global economy until the banks returned to health, and lines of credit and investment reopened. Governments that had nationalized banks wanted to sell them again in order to recoup some of the costs of having acquired them. The banks could only return to profit if they were able to earn money from investments; and the best way they had learned to do that was to keep investing in unstable secondary markets. Further, in seeking advice on how to regulate the highly complex activities that constitute the modern financial system, public authorities are dependent on the sector itself. This is a well-known theme in political science, known as regulatory capture: when those being regulated secure control of the regulatory process.

There have been some reforms. The Basel Committee on Banking Supervision (BCBS) – an international committee of central banks and banking supervision authorities – is toughening the rules on banks' capital adequacy ratios (the relationship between a bank's assets and the speculative trades it conducts). But these measures have been weak. The BCBS lacks international statutory powers, and in any case tends to stay as close as it can to the neoliberal rule that the markets know better than public authorities. It uses measures of risk developed by banks themselves and by the private credit ratings agencies that were among those responsible for failing to appreciate the extent of banks' problems in 2007. During the Obama administration in the US, there was an attempt to get tougher. The Dodd–Frank Act of 2010 raised capital holdings requirements on banks and regulated their risky investment activities. However, early in the life of the Trump administration (June 2017), Congress voted to weaken many of Dodd–Frank's provisions. Similarly, plans for a financial transactions tax (designed to reduce extreme velocity of financial transactions) by the EU have been watered down following intensive lobbying by the financial sector. (For a detailed account, see Lisa Kastner's 2017 study.) Meanwhile, investment firms that are not banks (such as hedge funds) are not covered by these attempts at regulation, even though their behaviour contributes heavily to instability.

Neoliberals argue that these post-2008 attempts to rein in bank irresponsibility, weak though they are, serve only to hamper trading, making it more difficult to share risk, and therefore hinder innovative activity. They might also point out that the types of investor who manage to stand outside the short-term share price model, such as venture capitalists, depend on an ability to keep some funds in volatile markets in order to have the resources for longer-term projects. But these advantages have to be set against the overall loss in welfare that occurs when an inadequately regulated system collapses, as it did in 2008. It can justifiably be claimed that the expectation that governments would bail banks out – that they were 'too big to fail' – encouraged them to take irresponsible risks, and that the post-2008 bailouts will only give banks incentives to take even bigger risks in the future. Bankers were also said to be 'too big to jail' when it became clear that none of those responsible for the disaster would be punished. But here too one has to set the damage done by bailouts against the danger of a total collapse of the global economy had nothing been done to stem the haemorrhage of share values that was taking place.

There has been a different experience with the post-2008 submission of banks to statutory 'stress tests'. Central bank officials test the ability of banks to be able to confront a range of shocks. If they fail the tests, they can be required to change their capitalization base or seek a merger with another bank. Such tests have been tough, and have been required by the European Central Bank (ECB), the US Federal Reserve Bank and the Bank of England. Banks have welcomed these tests, as they protect the system itself from risky banks. A collapse of banks' confidence in each other had been a major feature of the immediate aftermath of the crisis. The restoration of trust has also been a major concern of the ECB's financial compensation scheme (a similar measure has been introduced by the Bank of

England). This is designed to restore the confidence in financial institutions of small savers. Banks are required to contribute to an insurance scheme, which compensates investors in financial firms up to a maximum of €100,000. Banks and others do not oppose this and contribute to the insurance scheme because they know that, in the absence of something of this kind, in the wake of another crisis they would have difficulty persuading small wealth holders to part with their money. These are interesting examples of reforms to the neoliberal model that seem to require state (i.e., central bank) initiative and therefore external regulation, but that help preserve the market economy.

What Does 2008 Tell Us About Post-Democracy?

The differences in the finance industry's responses to the various post-crisis initiatives are in line with what we should expect under post-democracy: where a public policy provides financial firms with assurances that help themselves, it is welcomed; where it seeks to restrain their risk-taking that might damage the wider public, they oppose it, even though they might seem to have a long-term interest in such measures. The problem is that in responding to the 2008 crisis neither banks nor governments had a strong interest in the long term. Banks wanted to get back to making very large profits out of high-risk activity; if they can make enough money in a short period, they can probably sit back on their piles of wealth when the next crash comes. Also, since the sector as a whole, including certain banks within it, is essential to the functioning of the system, public authorities considered that they had to bail them out at public expense if they failed. They were then desperate for banks to get back to being profitable as soon as possible, so that the bailouts could end. The quickest route to that was through tolerating a return to high-risk lending.

The 2008 Financial Crisis

There is indeed evidence that risky finance in secondary markets, including sub-prime mortgages in the US, has returned. Banks learned after 2008 just how dependent on them we have become, and how far governments are willing to go to protect them from the consequences of their misdeeds. Moral hazard has intensified. Also, in more recent years there have been major advances in the digitalized share trading mentioned above. It is now possible for very wealthy investors to use equipment that can detect minuscule share movements and buy and sell in fractions of a second. While this can be seen as making trading more efficient, it can also be used in a parasitical way. Imagine two finance houses. House A starts to buy a particular stock. House B does not want this stock, but has faster computers than A. These detect that A is buying the stock, and use their speed to buy the stock before A can get to it. B then sells the stock to A at a higher price. There has been no general gain, but B has made money at the expense of A. This kind of trading, responding massively to very slight changes in prices, can produce exaggerated movements in share prices that could trigger unnecessary crises.

As Gordon Brown (2018) warned in an interview with the British Broadcasting Corporation (BBC), it is unlikely that the high level of intergovernmental cooperation that reined in the 2008 crisis and protected us from a repetition of 1931 would be achieved today. Partly as an ironic consequence of 2008, governments in several countries are more likely to insist on protecting their national interests at the expense of others. In particular, the US administration of Donald Trump has signalled its intention of withdrawing from many forms of international collaboration, especially in the economic field. China, the main target of Trump's protectionist policies, may now well be less willing to help the US than it was after 2008. The UK has withdrawn from the extensive cooperative frameworks of the EU. Russia is similarly less willing to participate in shared international activities, and at the time of writing nationalistic parties are dominating governments in Hungary and Poland.

The steps that led to the 2008 crisis, oversaw its rescue and continue to make financial markets unsafe fit very closely the model of post-democratic policymaking. (See, in particular, Greta Krippner's 2012 study of the politics of financial deregulation.) The world of revolving door personnel, moving from banks to government and back again, that characterizes US politics in particular, was a fairly perfect example. Several of the key figures involved from the 1980s onwards in dismantling the post-1931 system of US banking regulation worked for investment banks and hedge funds either before or after serving in the Treasury Department. In several cases, they both came from the sector and returned to it after they had changed the law to make investment more profitable and more risky. Goldman Sachs, the world's largest investment bank, featured particularly prominently in this process. Several of its senior executives have served as Secretaries to the Treasury, for Republican and Democratic administrations alike. In much of Europe, too, the ideas of Third Way social democracy led even governments of the centre left to prefer to spend their time with and listen to the spokespersons of large corporations than the people they claimed to represent.

My original account of post-democratic policymaking was over-simple in talking generally of economic elites and missed the differences that exist in corporate political power in different sectors. As we saw in the previous chapter, the sectors that are usually seen as of strategic importance – such as energy, mass-distribution food, armaments, pharmaceuticals and, also increasingly, IT – are also those with the oligopolistic tendencies that favour corporate political activism. But even these do not rival the politically privileged position of the financial sector. Its product is money itself, the lifeblood of the economy. While this has long been true, it has become more so as innovations in trading like those discussed above have increased the returns to financial activities above virtually everything else, and as deregulation has made governments eager to offer financial operators whatever they demand in order to attract their investments. The most trenchant analysis of the implications for democracy of the dominance of finance is that provided by Wolfgang Streeck (2017 [2013]). He argues that modern 'democratic' governments are not responsible to their citizens alone, but to two *Völker*, or sets of people: *Staatsvolk* (state people) and *Marktvolk* (market people). The former are nationally grounded, act as citizens with citizens' rights, vote (periodically), express their concerns via 'public opinion' surveys, show loyalty and look to governments for some of the provisions of daily life. The latter are international, act as investors who make demands, operate (continuously) through auctions of public debt, express their concerns through interest rate movements, show varying and unreliable degrees of 'confidence' rather than loyalty and look to governments to service debts owed to them. Streeck is concerned, not so much with the familiar theme of corporate lobbies, but with the deeper transformation of state responsibilities produced by the rise in public debt. More specifically, he considers the transition from the taxation state (*Steuerstaat*) to the debtor state (*Schuldenstaat*). The former has a primary relationship to its citizens (the *Staatsvolk*), from whom it requires consent to levy taxation. The debtor state, while maintaining this link, acquires a second one, which also serves, like taxation, as a major source of funds: the global financial markets from which it borrows money – hence responsibility to the *Marktvolk*. The preference of neoliberal policymakers for low taxation has increased governments' dependence on debt to fund their public spending programmes. Meanwhile, the rise of secondary markets has enabled financial institutions to accept even risky state debts, just as they accepted risky private debts. The more governments have had recourse to debt, therefore, the more powerful the *Marktvolk* have become, and the less responsive governments are able to be to their citizens, the *Staatsvolk*.

Would stronger democracy have performed better?

The 2008 crisis therefore revealed both that the general trend towards post-democracy was intensified by the changing role of finance, and that this key sector of neoliberalism was escaping market rules. But would things have been any different had both democracy and true market forces been stronger? This is necessarily a thought experiment, but one worth making.

We can reasonably contend that, had politicians been in more active, two-way contact with groups in society outside the financial elite, they would have been less ready to concede the banks' initial deregulatory demands. The regulations that were in place had mainly been erected after 1931 to protect society and the rest of the economy from dangerous behaviour in the financial sector. This was known history, not theoretical speculation. Had politicians in the 1990s been willing to listen to a wider range of opinion, and had so many US finance policymakers in particular not been part of the revolving door system, cautionary voices would surely have been more likely to have been heard, and deregulation would have proceeded more carefully. It is relevant that the deregulation process began in the US, where lobbying by very wealthy interests is more prominent than in most European societies. The UK, which during the 1980s had governments particularly concerned to privilege business interests and where labour had become singularly weak, followed rapidly. In other EU countries, where at that time political influence was more balanced across classes, deregulation at first moved more slowly. It gathered pace only when the US and UK seemed to be improving their overall economic performance because of it. Both individual governments and the EU itself began to follow the Anglo-American way. Further, in the wake of 2008 we might have expected a stronger move to re-regulation if interests other than those of finance had been able to wield more influence over governments.

There is also, however, hypothetical counterevidence to these arguments. The dominant wisdom among professional economists before 2008 was that the new approaches of the financial markets were risk-proof. This was embodied in the rational markets hypothesis, expounded in particular by Eugene Fama as long ago as 1970. This contended that share prices necessarily contained all relevant knowledge needed to make rational investment decisions. Another major American finance economist, Robert Shiller, argued against this that stock markets were vulnerable to 'irrational exuberance' (2000), and predicted the crises looming in US housing markets; but he was not heeded. Fama was saying what people wanted to hear; Shiller the opposite. Given the widespread preference among economists for arguments of Fama's kind, it was not unreasonable for nonexpert policymakers to have treated them as accepted wisdom. Even after the crash, proponents of Fama's theory continued to insist that they had been right, blaming government intervention that distorted markets as the cause of the crisis. Despite evidence that lack of knowledge on the part of investors had been an important element in the investments, particularly those in sub-prime mortgages, that had caused the crash, Fama was awarded the Swedish Central Bank's prize for economics (the so-called Nobel Prize for economics) in 2013. The prize committee did, however, also award the prize to Shiller.

We cannot confidently assert that fully democratically responsive politicians would have been more suspicious of the rational markets hypothesis and have the courage to listen to the wiser minority of unorthodox economists. After all, the problem of scarcity seemed to be being solved by the deregulation that had brought us the new secondary markets, and poor people were able to borrow money to buy homes and other major purchases in a way that had never before been possible. It could be argued that democracy had a duty to ensure that these possibilities were realized. It is therefore at least possible that even a more resilient democracy, sceptical of corporate lobbyists, would by itself not have avoided the financial crash. To do so, it would have needed support from two further elements: a richer diversity of expert advice, and less distorted markets.

Democracy should, in its own interests, never stint in its search for the best expert knowledge, even if today's right-wing populists have often successfully stigmatized expertise as elitist and therefore anti-democratic. Democracy should always want to get its decisions right; knowledge helps democracy to do this and is therefore always its friend. If democratic opinion insists that a bridge could be built in a way or at a cost that engineering knowledge indicates to be unsafe, democratic opinion should revise its view. There are, however, three problems with this dictum. First, knowledge in the social sciences, including economics, is less well established than in most of the natural sciences, where hypotheses can usually more easily be tested under laboratory conditions. Policymakers are therefore often confronted with disagreement among the experts they consult.

Second is the familiar problem of regulatory capture. Knowledge of a particular field is often monopolized by the interests active within it; authorities seeking to regulate the field in question need access to that knowledge to do so efficiently and this often means accepting the advice of those experts who serve the interests of those to be regulated. This problem, which applies to the natural sciences as much as to the social, is becoming more intense as knowledge becomes highly specialized and difficult for outsiders to comprehend, and as research in many areas becomes highly expensive, such that only corporations that stand to gain from exploiting the knowledge gained can afford to fund it. The case of the International Life Sciences Institute discussed in the previous chapter is a glaring example. Corporations do this in both their own laboratories and in university departments that they fund. Banks and other financial firms are highly active in using economists' expertise, in funding their research and in offering them well-remunerated jobs. Impartial expertise becomes ever harder to find, unless means can be found to strengthen the financing of truly independent research.

Third, the banking sector would not have created such political problems after 2008 had individual firms within it not been so large that they could present a systemic threat. For most of the above discussion we have considered problems of democratic weakness that produced excessive deregulation; here, we are more concerned with deregulation producing democratic weakness. Deregulation caused the crisis, at least in part; and widespread problems have resulted for democracy as a consequence. Democratic governments need to avoid becoming subordinated to systemic shocks produced by firms that are 'too big to fail'. There are two possible approaches to this. First, markets can be made more effective by preventing the formation of firms that can dominate markets, or breaking them up if they already exist. This is the classic antitrust approach of competition policy discussed in the previous chapter, and it is often used effectively by public authorities, especially the ECJ. Second, there are however sectors where this approach cannot be used, where size is so important to efficient functioning that breaking up corporations would have negative consequences, and where both entry to and exit from the market cannot be made easy. In these circumstances there is no alternative to either strong regulation or public ownership. One of the marks of post-democracy has been the removal of either or both of these safeguards in many sectors, most prominently finance.

Conclusion

'More democracy' alone would not have protected us from the 2008 crisis, as at every stage, from initial deregulation to coping with the aftermath of the crisis, politicians could reasonably argue that they were only doing what seemed best for their citizens, given the promise that a deregulated financial system seemed to be solving the age-old problem of scarcity. To have avoided the trap of deregulation, democracy would have needed support from outside itself. First, its representatives would have required access to diverse forms of expertise where there was controversy and the danger that a current orthodoxy was serving, or had been produced by, powerful interests. This, in return, would have required varied and independent financing of knowledge creation, greater suspicion of the role of corporations and other wealthy interests in funding research and knowledge dissemination, and a mass media and public opinion that took an intelligent interest in the products of that knowledge and debates surrounding it.

These are hard conditions to fulfil, given the complexity of so much knowledge and the low incentive that individual citizens have to acquire it, since a single voice is so infinitesimally small. However, societies with relatively democratic institutions do better in this regard than undemocratic ones. Only democracy can sustain a public arena in which contending bodies of knowledge can be examined. Even then, it is entirely possible that a well-informed democracy will make 'bad' choices. For example, the majority of a public fully and fairly informed about the risks to the environment posed by fossil fuels might still say: 'Why should I care about the world my grandchildren will inhabit in 30 years' time? I want cheap fuel for my car now.' That is a democratic decision, and can be criticized from a democratic perspective only if evidence has not been presented even-handedly and if powerful interests have swayed public debate predominantly on one side – as indeed they do. Growing corporate dominance of knowledge production and dissemination are making that problem worse. Beyond that, we cannot make the impossible stipulation that the unborn should have a vote. Democracy can look after future generations only if the living care about them. That is not impossible; people seem to express such care when they take great pains to pass on their wealth to their children and avoid death duties.

Democracy also needs support from the market, reducing the strain that can be imposed on it by dominant corporations, too big to fail and in highly imperfect competition. Democracy must always be open to lobbying; that is part of what a free society means. Problems occur when particular interests are so wealthy that they can wield a degree of pressure that others cannot rival and threaten systemic effects if their lobbying is not heeded. Small and medium-sized firms can do this only when they form associations, which brings its own difficulties. Most arguments about either combating or regulating monopoly and oligopoly are concerned with economic advantages and disadvantages; but there are also democratic ones. It may well be that we cannot have democracy without both a reduced level of inequality and also truly competitive markets.

4

The European Debt Crisis

The general financial crisis of 2008 demonstrated post-democracy in action, albeit with some important complexities and reservations. The treatment of debtor nations in the crisis of the common European currency, the euro, that followed from 2010 onwards, has often been presented as even worse, as a denial of democracy. It was not; but it was a clear instance of the practice of post-democracy and of the dominance of 'market people' over 'state people'. Even then, there were twists that prevent us from drawing what might seem to be the most obvious conclusions.

The main facts are as follows. As noted in the previous chapter, the sovereign debts of several states were among the unsafe assets in which investors had traded under the deregulated financial system. These played a similar role to the private debts of households with poor security. The banks now faced major losses, as these debts were revealed to be worthless. They could be saved from damage only if investors could believe that these state debts would be honoured. This was a subset of the general problem that a banking collapse would threaten the global economy unless governments bailed out the banks. Governments and citizens faced a sharp dilemma: either risk a global economic collapse or accept an obligation to repay debt. The latter would involve either major increases in taxation or major reductions in public spending, probably both. Whatever combination was chosen, such a sharp contraction in spending power would immediately cause reduced economic activity and therefore reduced capacity to repay the debts – a vicious spiral.

The situation of debtor countries in the Eurozone was particularly difficult. Management of a single currency that brings together a number of governments, each of which retains its own fiscal powers, is problematic. Either there are overall rules that partly limit governments' fiscal autonomy (so-called fiscal federalism), or reliance is placed on a single policy instrument. Disastrously, the founders of the euro chose the latter route, for two main reasons. First, governments preferred to maintain fiscal autonomy. The second reason was very different, but was made attractive by the fact that it was compatible with fiscal autonomy. Understanding it, and the subsequent development of the euro crisis, requires some background.

For reasons that will be explored below, German (earlier, West German) finance policy has been governed by the doctrine that a central bank must be politically independent and its sole objective must be to use its monetary policy to ensure a low level of inflation. Throughout extended discussions dating from the 1970s, West Germany had been reluctant to support the foundation of a single European currency, which was a central objective of successive French governments. The Germans feared that governments, particularly in southern Europe, would ignore its low inflation rule and undermine the stability of a shared currency. Since West Germany was the largest EU economy, the single currency project seemed doomed. However, after the fall of the Berlin Wall and general collapse of the Soviet bloc in eastern Europe, the West German government wanted to be allowed to absorb East Germany into a united German state. This would involve permitting the former East Germany to accede to the EU without having to join the queue of other states wanting to become members. If Germany could not reunite, the waves of immigrants coming from east to west would have imposed enormous burdens on the West German state, and left behind an impoverished, unstable East Germany. The French government offered to support German unification in exchange for West Germany accepting establishment of a single currency.

This left West Germany with little choice, but it also enabled it to take the lead in designing the rules for the ECB that would govern the euro, in particular the low inflation rule. This would leave individual governments free to determine their fiscal policy, provided they maintained low inflation. Acceptance of 'German' rules also played a major part in stabilizing the infant currency within the financial markets, there being considerable scepticism among global investors whether a transnational currency would be stable or even survive. Tough rules that would limit inflation would strengthen confidence following the currency's launch.

However, German finance policy has itself been full of ambiguities, which were then inherited by the euro. To understand what happened after 2010 in the Eurozone, it is necessary to have some knowledge of these. Almost alone among western countries recovering from the Second World War, West Germany had adopted a strong currency policy from the founding of the state in 1949. Elsewhere in western Europe, and also in North America, governments pursued policies associated with the British economist John Maynard Keynes of using fiscal policy to manage demand. When consumer demand was low, threatening recession, governments would increase their own spending and/or reduce taxes; when demand became so high that it threatened inflation, governments were supposed to reduce their spending and/or increase taxes. The aim was that budgets would be balanced over the long term, but some observers, especially in the financial markets, were sceptical whether governments would have the courage to reduce spending and increase taxes when necessary, leading to fears that, for political reasons, a Keynesian economy would have a higher level of inflation than others.

Germany had experienced particularly high levels of inflation in the years preceding the rise of Adolf Hitler, leading post-war West German policymakers to be particularly averse to any policies that might increase inflation. They therefore established the tough monetary policy that, in the following decades, was associated with German economic success, and was then passed on to the new common European currency.

But things were not that simple. West Germany did in fact begin to adopt Keynesian demand management in the late 1960s when it experienced its first post-war recession. Even before then, German financial policy benefited from Keynesian approaches in its European neighbours and in the US during the initial period of post-war recovery. As a result of the devastation produced by the defeat of the Nazi regime, Germans were extremely poor; the economy had little capacity for domestic consumption, and West German industry began its recovery with export sales, made possible at least in part by the fact that Keynesian demand management was sustaining consumer confidence in its key trading partners. The West German 'economic miracle' was therefore not really an example of how economic success can be independent of demand management. Also, it cannot provide a general model for other countries to follow: by definition, it is not possible for all to have export-led growth.

There is something equally mythical about German claims that a hard money policy had been central to West German economic success. Under the Bretton Woods system, described in the previous chapter, currencies did not float in the money markets, but were fixed in relation to the US dollar unless changed by governments. This was done only rarely, when an economy's performance had led the value of its currency to become seriously out of line. Emerging from wartime defeat, West Germany established a new currency, the *Deutsche Mark*, which was initially fixed at an extremely low exchange rate. As the economy embarked on its rapid growth path, the *Mark* experienced a series of upward revaluations, leading it to become one of the most stable hard currencies in the world. However, because its market value was rising continuously, while its revaluations took place only occasionally (in 1961 and 1969), for most of the time it was undervalued, and therefore not really a hard currency at all.

After the US engineered the collapse of Bretton Woods in 1972 in order to devalue the dollar, the world's major currencies floated on the market, and the *Mark*'s level rose, threatening Germany's export competitiveness. By 1979, the instability of the free-floating system had become unsustainable, as investors speculated on the potential weakness of this or that currency. The European Economic Community (as the EU was then called) established the Exchange Rate Mechanism (ERM) as a means of allowing limited floats among its member currencies. Governments and central banks would have to use interest rates to maintain a stable, though not fixed, level of their currency. The ERM was unable to protect the currencies of weak economies from extreme speculative pressure, sometimes requiring countries to raise interest rates to punishingly high levels. For example, this happened to the UK in 1992, forcing it out of the ERM.

The architects of the ERM had seen it as a precursor of European monetary union, though, until the events surrounding German unification described above, the politically autonomous German central bank, the Bundesbank, had always been very reluctant to accept that step. When the euro was finally launched in 1999, it brought an end to currency turmoil, not only among its member states, but more generally, as it created a large zone within which speculative trading in national currencies could no longer take place.

The European Debt Crisis

Alongside protection from speculative attacks on weaker economies, the euro imposed a complex pattern of obligations and advantages on its member economies. Governments and central banks lost the ability to set their own interest rates. Instead the ECB set a general rate reflecting overall conditions in the Eurozone. This meant that the weaker economies, mainly those in southern Europe, could benefit from a lower interest rate than would have been the case had they maintained their own currencies. As a result, these countries' firms were able to sustain higher levels of investment, and their economies grew faster. By the same token, stronger economies, especially Germany, had to accept a higher interest rate than their economies merited, which slowed their growth. At the same time, the young euro floated downwards in the currency markets, as external investors were sceptical of the project. This once again enabled Germany (and other strong Eurozone economies) to have an undervalued currency as in the early decades of the *Deutsche Mark*, boosting its export performance. But the weaker economies had to try to compete with export prices higher than they would have maintained if they still had their own weaker currencies.

In the wake of the Eurozone crisis of 2010, it has generally been forgotten that most informed opinion in the southern European countries had actively sought that last eventuality. For example, the role of several sectors of the Italian economy within the rather closed European market of the earlier EEC had been to provide cheap goods to northern Europe: for example, clothing and textiles, mass assembly white goods, as well as high-quality goods (such as machine tools and motor vehicles) that were cheaper than those being produced in northern Europe. The cost advantage was initially achieved by having lower real wages than the north, but as Italy became more prosperous the wage gap declined. The cost advantage was maintained by recurrent devaluations of the lira. Italy, as a founder member of the EEC, had sustained this strategy the longest, but it was joined by Greece, Portugal and Spain when those countries became members. By the 1990s it was clear that the low-cost strategy was becoming unsustainable. The arrival of the formerly state socialist countries of central Europe on capitalist world markets and eventually within the EU itself meant the entry of new competitors whose workers were accustomed to far lower wages than in most of the west. Whatever the deficiencies of state socialism, it had produced important engineering and similar skills. These could rival Italian and Spanish producers in engineering sectors. Almost at the same time, the international Multi Fibre Agreement was coming to an end. Established in 1974, this had erected tariffs against producers of clothing and textile goods in the Far East in order to protect these industries in western countries. The Agreement was gradually phased out, finally terminating at the end of 2004. This had been a particularly important sector for the southern European economies.

The south had lost its role as Europe's cheap producer. Especially in Italy, policymakers, business leaders and trade unions alike saw the solution as forcing producers to move up-market into high value-added products, competing on quality rather than price. Joining the euro was seen as assisting this strategy: no longer could devaluation be used to ensure price competitiveness; instead, economies would be tied to a common currency that overpriced their exports, imposing pressure on them to improve efficiency and quality.

The logic behind the foundation of the euro therefore seemed to meet the needs of all participating economies: all were spared the disruption of speculative attacks on various national currencies; Germany and other strong economies gained competitiveness from participating in a currency that was for them undervalued; weaker economies benefited from lower interest rates than their own economies would merit, and received an incentive to move up-market and abandon their no longer viable place in the wider European economy.

The flaw in the system was the narrow economic theory that governed it. Firms in the southern economies were expected to respond more or less automatically to the negative incentive of rising costs produced by abandonment by their governments of the recurrent devaluation strategy. To be truly effective, this strategy needed to be accompanied by government policies to improve infrastructure, training, business development advice and other public services. There was some response of this kind, particularly in Spain, and the EU itself has assisted southern regions with major transport and other infrastructure projects. But in general, politics in these countries, especially Greece and Italy, was dominated by clientelism and, often, corruption. During the military dictatorship from 1967 to 1974, Greek shipowners – the country's wealthiest and most profitable sector – had been granted permanent immunity from taxation; no subsequent democratic government felt able to challenge this, both main parties and the mass media being heavily dependent on shipowners for funding. In Italy, the governments of Silvio Berlusconi, the country's wealthiest man, were dominated by a need to pass laws exempting him from prosecution for various alleged offences in his business and private life.

The German government had been reluctant to have countries with problems join the euro, and had insisted that economies had to pass certain tests of solvency before they could do so. This conflicted with the desire of both the European Commission (EC), the executive branch of the EU, and the French government to ensure the new currency's stability by having its zone as large as possible. There was therefore some ambiguity over the strictness of the admission tests. Italian institutions set about ensuring that their country met the formal requirements, but we now know that the Greek government ensured entry by distorting some statistics.

A further instance of the naivety of the purely economics approach taken in the establishment of the euro was the belief that, provided countries met the constraint of keeping inflation below a certain level, restraining public debt, no other variables required attention. This meant that the ECB had no capacity to determine whether debt was being used for constructive purpose (such as to fund infrastructure or education) or merely to enable governments to increase pensions or other benefits without raising the taxes needed to fund them. It was also prevented by its 'German' rules from using Keynesian discretion, and was therefore unable to decide whether at certain conjunctures a temporary expansion of debt might be less damaging than moving into recession. Governments liked the arm's length relationship between their fiscal policy and the ECB, but the eventual effects on them were probably more severe than would have been produced by a degree of fiscal federalism. Even France and Germany failed to meet their inflation target at some point. The ECB turned a blind eye, not so much because their actions could have been judged to be wise avoidance of recession, but because these economies were too big to discipline.

While many observers saw that the euro incorporated serious design faults, hardly anyone appreciated the main force that would undermine it. This was the system of irresponsible debt trading encouraged by financial deregulation that was discussed in the previous chapter. Provided they were keeping inflation low, governments could maintain high levels of debt by trading it on the money markets. They therefore joined sub-prime house buyers in fuelling the debt-trading system. Following the 2008 financial crash, investors became deeply wary of all unsecured debt, whether of households or of states, and banks holding large quantities of it were vulnerable to collapses of confidence. As so often with financial markets, the issue was one of perception. If investors regarded an economy as being basically stable, a high level of debt did not create a confidence crisis in the banks that had accepted its debt; if it was seen as weak, then a crisis was likely. This explains why, although Spanish public debt was lower than that of Germany, Spain was deemed to have a debt crisis while Germany was not.

Attention focused on the countries of southern Europe and Ireland. In 2010, it became clear that banks that held the debt of these countries were in danger of collapse, potentially provoking a renewed global banking crisis. The European institutions (the ECB and the EC) and the IMF (since this crisis had global implications) moved to impose debt repayment conditions on the governments concerned in order to restore confidence in their creditor banks. This group was dubbed the 'troika', after the three-horse Russian sledge. But at least in the Greek case, there was a fourth horse, never officially mentioned. As Aditya Chakrabortty (2012) revealed, the International Institute for Finance (IIF), a lobby group representing 450 private banks across the world, was an active participant in the discussions of the troika over setting the terms of bank involvement. 'The four horsemen of the apocalypse' would have been more appropriate both numerically and in terms of mood than the jolly analogy of the troika.

While normal Eurozone procedures had concentrated on inflation and had left governments to pursue their own fiscal policies, the conditions imposed on the southern countries and Ireland firmly expressed a neoliberal ideology. The emphasis had to be on reductions in public spending, not increases in taxation. This was particularly explicit in the case of Greece, the country with the highest debt levels. The terms of its deal – as set out in the Memorandum of Understanding of February 2012 (Government of Greece 2012) – required the country to dismantle most labour market regulation and protection, and to reduce both the role of collective bargaining (and therefore of trade unions) in setting minimum wages and also labour market protection. The main aims of the labour market sections of the conditions were to expose workers to the full force of global labour market competition, requiring the country to compete on low prices alone; there was now no mention of the original strategy of up-skilling and improving the quality of the labour force that had justified the southern countries joining the euro in the first place. The only interest shown by the troika in infrastructural issues such as transport and energy was to ensure their privatization, and, thereby, profit-making opportunities for northern European corporations. The Memorandum showed no substantive interest in up-grading as such.

True, the terms of the Greek bailout included some valuable reforms to require the efficient functioning of public institutions – an important issue in that country. There were also items that were unwelcome to the country's wealthy elite, such as major drives against tax evasion, corruption and making excessive profits in the provision of pharmaceuticals. Further requirements for the reform of how the main professions conducted their business matched both neoliberal and social democratic agendas. But the main burden of a cost-reduction strategy fell on ordinary working people, particularly public employees, who were among the relatively few who could not engage in tax evasion. Whether the rich and Greece's exceptionally large numbers of self-employed would pay full taxes, and whether corruption would be rooted out and major efficiency gains made in public services, was far more doubtful. Given that Greece has to continue to buy raw materials and semi-finished goods on world markets, it is only labour and social policy costs that can be reduced to achieve price competitiveness. Greek workers were reduced either to fighting defensive battles to protect rights that in themselves would achieve little that was oriented to the future, or to accepting years of austerity until their labour costs could compete with those of eastern Europe or the Far East.

A further Greek Memorandum, signed in 2015, showed that some learning had taken place within the troika. There was more emphasis on broadening the tax base and on constructive policies. Also, more generally, the rules governing the euro had changed during the course of managing the crisis. Some of these impose even tougher constraints on public spending, but at least recognize that a currency cannot be managed through inflation targets alone. There has also been a move to more flexibility.

This, however, is for the future. Our interest here focuses mainly on the allegation that management of the 2010 Eurozone crisis itself was anti-democratic, let alone post-democratic. Governments were required to accept tough packages of spending cuts imposed by the European troika (and, de facto, by the IIF) or withdraw their currencies from the euro. Such restored national currencies, losing all shield against market speculation, would clearly have fallen to extremely low levels. It is sometimes argued, especially by British opponents of the existence of the euro, that this liberation from a German-determined currency would have given them an immediate boost in competitiveness, restoring them rapidly to prosperity. This hypothesis ignores several factors. First, in addition to providing cost advantages, a currency devaluation produces price increases on all imports, generating inflation. A moderate devaluation might still be worth risking, but these economies would have faced a likely total collapse of their currencies, especially in contemporary financial markets, where leveraged loans can finance major exercises in shorting. Also, within the integrated economies of the contemporary world, many components of both goods and services incorporate inputs from other countries. For example, the OECD (2017) has calculated the import content of exports for a wide range of countries, showing that even for large economies this can be high. This reduces considerably the competitiveness gain from devaluation. Not surprisingly, none of the governments concerned wanted to take those risks. Both they and their publics were determined to remain within the single currency.

In two cases – Greece and Italy – the governments in office (the Greek one of the centre left, and the Italian of the centre right) refused to accept the troika's terms. The troika therefore proposed the appointment of replacement prime ministers – both former employees of Goldman Sachs – and invited the respective parliaments to choose between accepting the new governments or dropping out of the euro. In both cases they chose the former. These governments were temporary, and, in Greece, a general election in 2015 produced one dominated by a new left-wing party, Syriza, which was opposed to the troika's terms. It held a national referendum on whether it should accept the terms, and its ministers attended the next meeting of the troika armed with a strong mandate to reject it. The troika was unmoved; Greece submitted to the terms. Within the same year, Syriza called another general election, and remained the largest party until defeated in a normal general election in 2019.

The Handling of the Eurozone Crisis and Post-Democracy

Management of the Eurozone crisis bore all the hallmarks of policymaking under post-democracy. As with the 2008 financial crisis discussed in the previous chapter, priority was placed on saving the banks, ordinary workers had to bear the burden and governments had to take the unpopular measures of imposing harsh measures on their citizens. The banks, whose irresponsible lending had helped produce the crisis, had to accept some limitations on their expectations of repayment (what the German chancellor Angela Merkel called a 'haircut'), but otherwise escaped major damage. Greece and the other debtors were not allowed to default on their debts while continuing to function, as some forms of bankruptcy law permit firms to do. The German public was not even made aware that, in having to offer 'help' to Greece, they were actually bailing out the German banks on which their own savings depended. They preferred resentfully to see this as help being given to 'lazy Greeks'.

Much has been made of the fact that the German words for debt and guilt are the same – *Schuld*. But the word for creditor – *Gläubiger* – also has a second meaning: one who believes (the word 'creditor' derives from the Latin word for believe, *credo*). Normally, those who choose to believe are considered to share responsibility for that belief with those in whom they believe. Loans are the shared risk of lender and recipient, and strict accounting theory makes both of them responsible for the risk, so that both have an incentive to act prudentially (Amato and Fantacci 2012 [2009]; 2014 [2012]). But prudence does not feature in the lexicon of the main movers in contemporary money markets. Indeed, they seemed to be able to demonstrate in the Greek crisis that they were not only 'too big to fail', but also too big to share responsibility for their own behaviour.

The institutions of the troika that formally managed the crisis were only indirectly democratic. The ECB, the EC and the IMF are deemed to be democratic because they derive their mandates from governments that are themselves democratically elected, but that kind of indirect democratic reckoning is very typical of post-democracy, where democratic form is all important, its substance kept as small as possible. The directly elected European Parliament played no role at all. The more or less secret participation of the IIF was also pure post-democracy, the silent insinuation of private and partial business interests into public decision-making. New prime ministers (ex-bankers) were temporarily imposed on Greece and Italy, but their parliaments were required to give them a typically post-democratic formal endorsement. The Greek people were allowed to elect a new government to replace the one that had been imposed, but their rejection in a referendum of the terms of the troika's memorandum was ignored.

Management of the Eurozone crisis was certainly a powerful illustration of post-democratic practice. On the other hand, as we did at the end of Chapter 3, we must ask what an alternative democratic approach to the problem might have looked like. The main reason for the non-involvement of the EU's directly democratic institution, the European Parliament, was that the UK government, although not a member of the Eurozone, had vetoed its participation as part of the UK's own growing hostility to all EU institutions. The rejection of the democracy of the Greek referendum can be explained by the fact that Greece was requiring assistance from the other countries of the Eurozone if it was to remain within the zone. The Greek public could not reasonably expect to be able to vote on how this should be done without the citizens of the rest of the zone having a similar vote. Let us therefore imagine that the European Parliament had been involved, and that referenda on the deal had been held throughout member countries. It is just possible that the Parliament might have voted for a more creative and helpful rescue package; the German trade union confederation, the Deutsche Gewerkschaftsbund, did indeed propose a 'Marshall Fund' approach to the southern countries, but few other institutions outside the south joined its call. There might have been at least an extension of the debt repayment period, which is what eventually happened, though only after much suffering had been imposed on the populations of the debtor countries. A less bank-dominated decision structure might well have reached that position sooner. However, it is unlikely that citizens of countries where the creditor banks were located would have voted that their banks (and therefore their own savings) should take a bigger hit in order to help the countries in crisis.

The troika's requirement that the prime ministers of Greece and Italy be replaced was anti-democratic, post-democratically legitimated. However, neither of the deposed prime ministers concerned can be held up as fine examples of democracy. The case of Silvio Berlusconi in Italy was discussed in Chapter 1. His pattern of parties being formed by wealthy individuals who then become their leaders has been a characteristic of political systems in other parts of the world where civil society is weak and unable to generate strong movements from below. It became an important phenomenon in central Europe after the first pro-democracy movements weakened during the 1990s. Until the arrival of Syriza and some other new movements, Greek parties of centre left and centre right alike have been dominated by shipping industry interests, as noted above, and they have continued the privileges of that sector. Had its enormous earnings been correctly taxed over the decades, Greece might well have avoided its large debts. While it is certainly true that the troika's actions in having parliaments ratify the temporary external imposition of leaders were instances of post-democracy, they replaced regimes that were themselves post-democratic. In both countries, governments had taken on high levels of debt in order to fund electorally popular social programmes without being willing to fund them through taxation. These policies were not examples of Keynesian demand management, but chronic debt incurred through cynical manipulation of electorates through an indefinite postponement of an inevitable reckoning. It is very difficult for even strong democracy to deal unaided with manipulation of this kind.

Critics of the single currency argue that, had the debtor countries never entered it, they would have been able to manage their financial affairs through their own democratic institutions and thereby avoid the distress to which their populations were subjected after 2010. To appraise this, we need to consider how their debts would have progressed had they been outside the Eurozone. They would probably still have been able to fund their public debt through the secondary markets, which, as we have seen, were eager to accept any debt, and after 2008 would have suffered the shock of the collapse of these markets. Instead of this producing a crisis for the whole Eurozone and the consequent intervention of the troika, the individual countries would have suffered a catastrophic collapse of their national currencies, going way beyond the 'adjustment' that advocates of devaluation usually believe to be possible. Such collapses usually lead governments around the world to seek the aid of the IMF, which offers support in exchange for the acceptance of conditions to remedy the debt. Since the IMF was part of the troika, it is not clear that the proscribed medicine would have been so different from what occurred.

European Post-Democracy

The European debt crisis demonstrated a number of major institutional weaknesses. One is the problem at national level of governments pursuing unsustainable combinations of high spending and low taxation. Both democracy and post-democracy are likely to facilitate such practices, as they help governments to be popular. This returns us to the fundamental issue of how democratic citizens can be protected from various kinds of abuse by those they elect. One could give a facile answer: that in a strong democracy citizens are alert to all malpractices and punish them; that it is therefore only in post-democracy that this weakness is a problem; and that strengthening democracy would strengthen citizens' resistance to political malpractice. But this is naive. Even in a strong mass democracy, citizens may often vote to have their cake and eat it – high spending with low taxes. This leads us, as in Chapter 3, to consider the role of institutions that protect democracy from those elected in its name. The weaker that democracy is itself, the more important become such institutions. Protection of an institution can come only from outside it; democracy needs institutions to protect it that are not themselves democratic, but that have mandates given to them by democratic governments. This paradox makes them vulnerable to attack, and for their opponents to be able to claim that overriding such institutions strengthens democracy. We shall continue this discussion in later chapters. A second set of weaknesses was the deregulated financial system that enabled countries to trade in excessive debt in the first place. Here, the Eurozone crisis was just a subset of the wider crisis discussed apropos the financial crisis in Chapter 3, and shares in the analysis of the role of post-democracy established there. Finally come the design weaknesses of the single currency itself. As discussed above, these resulted from the systematic errors of a purely economics approach to the politics of finance, combined with certain specificities of German financial history, but also from a need to ensure that the new currency could sustain a strong position on global currency markets. One can speculate whether a more vibrant democracy at the European level would have resulted in a more flexible form of a European single currency, but behind that imponderable lies a bigger but more resolvable problem: the democratic status of EU institutions. As the crisis has continued to develop, the ECB has had to change its role and now assumes more general responsibilities. It more closely resembles a true central bank rather than a single-index monetary regulator. These have, however, been incremental movements responding to logjams, usually with the main priority of encouraging certain kinds of behaviour in banks, which have therefore been the main beneficiaries. There needs now to be a proper assessment of the ECB's responsibilities towards the European economy, including the impact its actions are having on north–south divergences. Valuable proposals have been made by the Hans Böckler Stiftung, the think-tank attached to the German trade unions (Watt and Watzka 2018). Such reforms would necessarily involve moving outside the neoliberal framework, and towards a more integrated European economy.

In *Post-Democracy* I described the European Parliament as a more or less pure instance of post-democracy. It has all the attributes of democracy: elections, changing majorities, debates and controversies. Yet it is not at all deeply rooted in the hearts and minds of European citizens.

Participation in its elections is poor and – until the election of 2019 – declining. Although there are cross-national party groups, they have little wider meaning; voters are usually voting for a national party rather than for a wider European entity. Unlike nearly all European national parliaments, the de facto government of the EU is not elected from the Parliament but is a separate institution. The EC is not responsible to the Parliament, which has a role but no final say in what emerges as European law. The office of President of the Council was an invention of the Treaty of Lisbon in 2007. It is held by a politician, and represents the ensemble of member governments. It was established to offset the non-democratic impression given by the President of the Commission, previously the most prominent EU individual, being the head of the bureaucracy. However, both presidents are elected by the governments of the member states, and are therefore examples of only indirect democracy. Indirect democracy – selection by a group that is itself directly elected – is not a creation of post-democracy, but it is particularly suitable (or vulnerable) to post-democracy, as the public is kept at a distance from substantive engagement, while the formal roots of the procedure can be justified as democratic.

Some observers have seen in the hobbled nature of EU democracy a political design on the lines of Friedrich von Hayek's ideas of transnational institutions that would remove economic decision-making from the reach of the democracy of the nation-state (Bonefeld 2017; Streeck 2015b). Hayek was a member of the ordoliberal school of Austrian and German economic philosophers who, starting during the Nazi period, sought to design a capitalist economy that would be autonomous, free from political interference of either the Soviet or the Nazi kind, or indeed of general democratic demands for protection of people's lives from the market's disruptions. Ordoliberals did not believe in an unregulated capitalism of the kind that later became dominant in American neoliberal theory, as they held that rules would always be necessary to maintain competition and to restrict the impact of markets on other areas of life. They were highly influential in establishing the rules of German finance policy with which we have been concerned in this chapter. Hayek himself was also later a major personal influence on the thinking of Margaret Thatcher and Ronald Reagan, neoliberal British prime minister and US president, respectively.

Bonefeld and Streeck both argue that the EU's weak and indirect democratic institutions fit Hayek's preferences. They therefore see the shift of political decision-making from nation-states to the EU as a weakening of democracy – or, one might say, an intensification of the post-democratic trends already developing at national level. Streeck in particular has gone on to argue that the demolition of the EU itself is necessary in order to restore democracy at the level where it has always been strongest: the nation-state.

There are two problems here, apart from the difficulty of transferring ideas formulated in Germany in 1939 to EU institutions of the twenty-first century. First, to present the EU as solely an embodiment of ordoliberal ideas, it has to be presented as an institution that insists almost solely on guaranteeing the competitive market, through institutions that are beyond democratic reach and with no forms of social or infrastructural policy. This describes an EU of the kind that had been wanted by British neoliberal nationalists, but it is precisely these people who have worked hard and successfully to bring the UK out of the Union. Either they have a completely inaccurate perception of the EU, or the image of it presented by Bonefeld, Streeck and some others is partial, concentrating on some albeit accurately described elements in EU behaviour, but ignoring others. It has to be the latter. Over the years, the EU has developed the democracy of its institutions and funded social and infrastructural projects that have in themselves redistributed resources from the northwest to the south and east of the continent. It is easy to sneer at the weakness of the European Parliament, but it remains the only example in the world of an attempt to create some transnational democracy. The powers of the Parliament have, over the years, been increased, and if they have not grown more rapidly it is because national politicians have been reluctant to share their place in the hearts and minds of European citizens, not because they have been reading Hayek. There is also European social policy, diminished and weakened in recent years, but still part of the *acquis communautaire*, the accumulation of policies that have to be adopted by new member states.

Second, the arguments of Bonefeld and Streeck assume that there could be a return to national economic sovereignty during a period when economic life has become increasingly global. This would require one of two sets of conditions. The first is that national democracy concern itself solely with those economic issues that it can handle alone, leaving issues that could be managed only transnationally to unregulated markets. The problem with this is that it accepts the essential post-democratic condition of a politics that cannot reach the levels where the most important developments are taking place – a situation with which Hayek would be very content.

The alternative is that countries cut themselves off from as much global commerce as possible, by erecting tariff and regulatory walls against others, by reducing exports and imports to a minimum, by restricting capital movements and by removing their currencies from market trading. There could then be a return to national economic sovereignty. Proponents of this approach regard it as returning to the initial Bretton Woods world: many national economies and the early EEC had tariff walls; governments restricted capital movements; currencies were fixed. But Bretton Woods envisaged and oversaw a liberalizing trend in world trade, out from the belligerent fortress economies of the 1930s towards more cooperation and international rules. Bretton Woods itself was an example of international economic regulation, as were the IMF, the OECD, the World Bank and other institutions established at that time. Tariffs were gradually being reduced under successive rounds of the General Agreement on Tariffs and Trade (GATT); capital movements were gradually being liberated. GATT eventually gave way to the more integrated governance of the World Trade Organization (WTO). To 'return' to the early Bretton Woods world would involve moves in exactly the opposite direction: the erection of hostile trading barriers against other nations, the demolition of international organizations, that process which President Trump has lauded as the triumph of patriotism over multilateralism and globalism. World trade would decline, and relations among nations become more dangerous. It is also worth reflecting that during the Bretton Woods period countries with social democratic governments (as in Scandinavia and from time to time the UK and Germany) were more likely to favour free trade than were those dominated by conservatives (France, Italy) or lingering fascism (Portugal, Spain).

Economic systems, like all systems that move through time, are incapable of simple 'returns' to a *status quo ante*. There is an important difference between a set of national economies that is moving towards integration and liberalization and one that is moving back towards disentanglement and the establishment of boundaries. This returns us to the image of the parabola discussed in Chapter 1, though applied here to international economic relations rather than to democracy. On one dimension, two points are at identical places, but on the time dimension they are located very differently. Given that human experience remembers (or tries to remember) where it has come from and what has happened to it, location in time is fundamental to the character of institutions.

In the advanced western world, the initial post-war decades saw a moving balance between democratic national control and liberal international engagement, a relatively benign liberal democracy that eventually, however, became loaded more heavily towards the international (indeed, global) and hence marked a decline of democracy. Movement in the opposite direction, currently taking off across major parts of the world, especially in the US, involves a series of unfriendly acts towards former allies and a rejection of institutions of international cooperation. When economies have become deeply entangled in cross-national supply chains, with corporations and investments spanning national boundaries, a de-globalization movement would require the severance of many of these relationships, with further disruption and increases in costs. The gains that usually flow from trade would be reduced. Poor countries joining the global trading system would confront new tariff barriers from the wealthy, setting back their development and the living conditions of their inhabitants, and intensifying divisions between rich and poor parts of the world.

A reversal of international integration would not 'return' us to the 1970s. The general context would be one of growing international hostility; income and wealth would decline as gains from trade were lost; technological developments that have reduced the manpower needed to produce certain goods and services would remain, preventing a return of the occupational structures that constituted the 1970s economy. As populations became more nationally conscious, they would grow in enmity towards, and suspicion of, foreigners of all kinds, including those living among them. Also, a world of autonomous, rarely cooperating, highly competing nation-states would do nothing about climate change, the gravest threat facing human life. The threats to our climate do not recognize national borders; tackling them requires cross-national cooperation. It is no coincidence that President Trump and those around him deny the reality of cross-national environmental dangers.

Issues of international banking regulation, fiscal evasion, tax rate competition and environmental threats require either impossibly sealed borders or cross-national institutions. Democracy is therefore between a rock and a hard place. We cannot recreate the world that existed before globalization, but globalization certainly takes us to political places where democracy is very weak. I have described elsewhere what I see to be the only way forward (Crouch 2018). First, we need a strengthening of world-regional institutions with a democratic component. The EU is the world leader here. The European Parliament may be weak and post-democratic, but it exists, and the EU is the only example of an elaborate system of cross-national cooperation that extends beyond trade relations to include labour conditions, social rights, health, safety and environmental standards, as well as cultural and scientific activities. This is a precious set of institutions. We need to find ways of rooting them more genuinely in the lives of Europe's citizens, not laugh at them for their democratic inadequacy.

However, many international issues – such as climate change – require global rather than world-regional action. But it is not possible to envisage a global set of democratic institutions. We can, however, demand a world in which national politicians freely admit that there are problems that are beyond their reach, that they need to cooperate with others within international agencies, and that therefore governments' policies within those agencies become fiercely debated within national politics. For example, is it unrealistic to imagine a general election in which an opposition party makes a major issue out of a government's failure to work with other countries within the WTO to suppress slavery, child labour and inhuman working hours? The international schoolchildren's movement for action on the climate change crisis that emerged during 2019 suggests that the next generation of citizens might demand an international politics of exactly that kind. Even without such democratic pressure, the OECD, the IMF and the World Bank are already beginning to see the limitations of their earlier neoliberal assumptions. They have changed their approach towards inequality, redistributive taxation and the need for constructive public action. They seem able to do this precisely because they have an international perspective and no political axes to grind. But because they occupy such a position, they also lack democratic legitimacy in a world where, outside the EU, there are no democratic institutions above national level. They need to be brought into democratic debate by national forums reaching out to them. The level of democracy in these institutions will always be weak, more like post-democracy than the real thing; but our choice is between that and a global economy with no democracy at all.

5
Politicized Pessimistic Nostalgia: A Cure Worse than the Disease

In recent years, movements have arisen in most European countries, the US and elsewhere that appear to share many of the complaints I made about contemporary democracies in *Post-Democracy* – in particular, criticisms of the dominance of politics by remote elites who seem to silence the voices of ordinary people. These are the so-called 'populist' movements. They come from the left, centre and right of the political spectrum, but by far the most important are those generally seen as of the right – the conservative rather than the neoliberal right – because their most distinguishing characteristic is to express nostalgia for a past that is slipping away. Mainstream political parties do not have much time for nostalgia, as they are constantly urging us to embrace change and what they see as progress. The new conservative movements fill the space that has been left by this process, embracing a golden view of a past, not necessarily an historical one, and presenting it as being threatened by invaders of a world that the nostalgic believe rightly belongs to them. The invaders most literally take the form of immigrants, especially practitioners of religions that dilute the nation's dominant faith. Also seen as invaders are international institutions that require nation-states to cooperate and pool elements of their sovereignty rather than express the pride of national separateness. New economic forces are also seen to be destroying old familiar industries and occupations. In a further example, women are presented not only as invading activities that used to be monopolized by men, but also as criticizing forms of behaviour that have been seen as expressing masculine pride. In each case, liberal attitudes are blamed for allowing the invasion, because liberalism implies the willing acceptance of diversity, and a liberal elite is attacked for fostering these attitudes and imposing them on an unwilling conservative people.

The importance of nostalgia and pessimism in distinguishing voters for xenophobic, far-right parties from others has been studied in depth with reference to eight west European countries in a prescient article by Eefje Steenvoorden and Eelco Harteveld, using data from 2012, an early point in the current xenophobic resurgence. The countries concerned were Belgium, Denmark, Finland, France, the Netherlands, Norway, Sweden and Switzerland. Nostalgia and pessimism were particularly strong among far-right voters in the Nordic countries and the Netherlands. The authors point out that various liberalizing movements have been generally stronger in those countries than in the other three. Since 2012, the range of countries to which the idea applies has grown considerably. Edoardo Campanella and Marta Dassù (2019) have applied it usefully to the emotions that led British voters to choose to leave the EU and US voters to elect Donald Trump as president.

These conservative movements give nostalgia political expression as a zero-sum game, a need to exclude and reject outsiders and newcomers in order to create space for the 'true' people in a shrinking world. (The most outstanding expression of such an outlook remains Adolf Hitler's justification for invading neighbouring countries on the grounds that the German people needed *Lebensraum* – living space.) This is an essentially pessimistic and bleak perspective. Immigration must be stopped. Nation-states must free themselves from attempts at international cooperation. The entry of new parts of the world into markets that used to be monopolized by the wealthy west must be restricted. Jobs in old familiar sectors should be protected from change. Women should return to their roles as mothers and housewives. The sexually unorthodox should not be allowed to express themselves. In Christian societies, the nostalgic believe that Christians should have superior religious rights over those of other faiths, and ought themselves to return to protecting their traditional values rather extending tolerance to various kinds of deviation from these. (In societies where Islam or some other religion has been historically dominant, one merely substitutes the religion in question for the word 'Christian' in that sentence.) An individual professing some of these attitudes may well not hold them all. It is, for example, entirely possible for feminist movements to be wary of extending a welcome to forms of Islam that keep women in very traditional roles. Similarly, several anti-Islamic movements make a feature of flying the Israeli flag (seen as a symbol of hostility to Arabs), while themselves also being very hostile towards Jews. But the political organizations that come forward to represent some of these resentments are themselves likely to signal, if sometimes tacitly, that they will offer sympathy and some favourable policies to all of them.

The necessary illiberalism of politicized pessimistic nostalgia means that it has anti-democratic tendencies, and for this reason can make only a limited contribution to the critique of post-democracy. Indeed, I shall argue here that its proffered cure for post-democracy is worse than the disease itself. I make my starting point politicized pessimistic nostalgia rather than either xenophobia or populism, the two terms that are mainly used. Xenophobia is certainly a key element in hostility to immigrants, to international cooperation and to the economic changes brought by globalization. However, one needs to move beyond this narrow characterization and take account of masculism and other forms of regret at change if one is to understand the depth of the appeal of these movements and the human feelings that lie behind them.

'Populism' is a problematic term, because it can simply refer to movements that are not contained within established political parties and that have themselves weakly structured, inchoate organizations. When they first appear, they behave in ways that challenge the established rules (formal and informal) of political conduct, but operate as the voice of their supporters, who are in general political outsiders having neither experience of nor respect for such rules. Populist movements burst uninvited, loudly and rudely, into a room where groups of people are having polite conversations. This is why they seem likely candidates to challenge post-democracy. Populism defined in this way may simply be the form taken by a new movement when it seeks inclusion in mainstream politics. Newcomers who lack prior invitations cannot enter a room without disturbance, and how is change in political representation and the renewal of democracy to take place without the occasional arrival of the uninvited? If an existing system of representation is wearing out, standing for social structures and issues of the past, renewal is bound to take forms disturbing to the parties of that system. We would know that post-democracy had fully arrived if existing parties so controlled a system that no such new movements could appear. Naturally, existing parties resent the intrusion and stigmatize the newcomers as populists – that is, movements that have no overall programme or roots in society, but that just exploit any available discontents in order to advance their own position. If populist movements are something more than that and represent interests that have been neglected, they will eventually become parties with structures and programmes; they will 'settle down' and take their place in the room, having made their mark and brought new issues to the political table.

In the purest case, populists claim to have no prior agenda of their own, but to be mere mouthpieces of the people. This is a naive approach, as it is not possible for 'people' to shape a political agenda without structured debate and extended discussion. A movement that claims to be no more than a mouthpiece is vulnerable to takeover by more organized groups. The Movimento Cinque Stelle (M5S) in Italy has been a fairly pure form of such a movement, developing policies through social media crowdsourcing on behalf of citizens discontented with the behaviour of the country's political elite. In government from 2018 to 2019 alongside a highly xenophobic party, La Lega, with which it originally did not have much in common, M5S was temporarily dragged towards the nationalistic right.

More common are movements that do have their own agendas. There can be populism of the centre. In the 2016 French presidential elections, all the established parties, together with the far-right populism of the Front National (FN), were swept aside by Emanuel Macron's centrist La République En Marche. Held together mainly by widespread aversion to the FN, there has been little to sustain its momentum beyond that election. Other populist movements have appeared from the political left. The most important examples have been in Latin America, where they have emerged in struggling, weak democracies and therefore hardly count as opponents of post-democracy. In Europe, the most important instances of leftist populism are Syriza in Greece, Podemos Unidos in Spain, La France Insoumise in France and Aufstehen in Germany.

Syriza, the only leftist populist party so far to have formed a government in a stable democracy (from 2015 to 2019), conducted itself within constitutional norms. It had brushes with the judiciary of a kind often associated with populism, but accepted the sovereignty of the courts.

For most of modern history, the left (both liberal and socialist) has been associated with 'progress' and looking forward. Conservatives are more concerned with the past. More recently, the decline of manufacturing industry and mining have produced grounds for nostalgia on behalf of the organized, manual, primarily male, working class – and hence for the left. If this leads parts of labour movements pessimistically to protect their past positions by seeking to exclude and to narrow down, they lose the openness and universalism that are core characteristics of the political left. If they seek defensively to protect systems that can offer the good things of life to only a few, they slip towards the conservative right, the proper home of exclusion and pessimistic nostalgia. It is notable that La France Insoumise, Aufstehen and parts of the left wing of the British Labour Party have started to adopt anti-immigrant and anti-European positions. The Danish Social Democratic Party has echoed anti-Islamic, but not anti-EU, positions.

Right-wing populism is, logically, by far the most significant home for pessimistic nostalgia, and it is currently the most rapidly growing form of politics. Ireland and Portugal are the only west European countries to lack the phenomenon; at the time of writing, right-wing populism dominates politics in Brazil, Hungary, India, Italy, Poland, Russia, Turkey, the UK and the US, and is growing in Bulgaria, Czechia, Slovakia and Slovenia. It has had periods as either minority parties in government or supporting centre-right governments in Austria, Denmark, Estonia, the Netherlands, Norway and Switzerland, and has been well established in France for considerably longer. Its relatively new parties have also made an impact on the politics of Belgium, Germany and Sweden. Its movements are not tied to particular socioeconomic groups. Much debate around them, among allies and opponents alike, presents them as representing the 'left behind', seeming to imply people likely to be poor and becoming economically marginalized. Such people may well be included, but feeling 'left behind' may often be the experience of people who have simply lost some previous privileges, or just think that they do not have privileges to which they feel entitled. 'Pessimistic nostalgia' captures all these possibilities, and not just the victims of economic decline. Indeed, since by definition the political right is anti-egalitarian, rightist populism has to define its enemies in terms other than wealth and power, and direct its antagonism instead against those groups, usually starting with immigrants and other ethnic minorities, who are seen as threatening the positions, or past positions, of those the populists seek to represent. We shall here be concerned only with these pessimistic and nostalgic forms of populism of the political right, which I shall also call by some of its advocates' own preferred name, the alt.right. This avoids confusion with other forms of populist politics.

Understanding Pessimistic Nostalgia

People with a conservative disposition, which includes nearly all of us at times, value stable, familiar things. When these seem to be lost to us, we experience nostalgia. In itself, nostalgia is a quiet sadness. It is not necessarily pessimistic or political, and can even be combined with a belief that new good things may replace the old that are fading away. However, when it is pessimistic and that pessimism is politicized, it can become aggressively possessive, identifying and directing anger against enemies who are accused of taking away the life that people remember as having been happier. The anger of pessimists has a different quality from that of those who believe they are being prevented by opponents from entering a new optimistic life that they have never enjoyed. It is necessarily defensive, exclusionary, potentially life-denying, and therefore liable to violent expression.

It is a deep irony of our period that, although Muslims have been one of the principal targets of this political mood in the western world, and the terrorist attacks of radical Islam have been probably the biggest single force propelling people towards the alt.right, radical Islam is itself the most extreme expression of pessimistic nostalgia. Al Qaida, the violent movement that for several years led radical Islam, called itself 'The army whose men love death'. There can be no greater expression of pessimism than that of the suicide bomber. Islamist groups do not share the concern for ethnicity or race of much western pessimistic nostalgia, because Islam (like Roman Catholicism) is not identified with particular ethnic groups. Otherwise, it has similar roots in resentment at existential threats to a treasured world, and the nature of perceived enemies is remarkably similar: atheists, practitioners of opposed religions or more liberal forms of Islam itself; modernizers and globalizers who spurn traditional ways and compromise cultural separatism; women who will not keep their place; the sexually unorthodox.

Both radical Islamists and western far-right leaders would insist that they are optimists, looking forward to a rebirth of old values. But the future to which they look forward involves a desire to return to a past, the search for a better yesterday. At the time of writing, the British Conservative government believes that, outside the EU, Britain will resume the global economic and military role it possessed when it had an empire. The Austrian far right party, the Freiheitliche Partei Österreichs (FPÖ), until recently in government, talks of building a special alliance with the central European countries that once formed part of Austria's empire. The governing party of Hungary, Fidesz, talks of restoring the 'greater Hungary' that formed part of the same empire. The Islamic State terrorist movement dreams of restoring the caliphate.

It is wrong to regard current alt.right movements as the equivalent of the fascist movements of the interwar years, as, with the exception of the Islamists, they do not openly espouse the violent elimination of opponents. They are, however, of the same political family: nationalistic, hostile to foreigners and to liberal values. Deep ambiguity about the relationship between past and future was also symptomatic of the fascist movements. Benito Mussolini's fascist party presented itself as future-oriented, and managed to co-opt the artistic movement of the Futuristi and to attract support from parts of the cultural *avant garde* in several other countries. However, particularly after his pact with the Vatican, Mussolini also imposed a return to many conservative social practices, including the place of women and hostility to foreigners. Adolf Hitler's Nazis were more obviously nostalgic – the idea of a Third Reich hearkened back to the Roman Empire of classical times and to the post-medieval Holy Roman Empire disturbed by Napoleon Bonaparte in the early nineteenth century. The Nazi regime reintroduced the old Gothic script of the German language in place of the modern, more readable forms that had been introduced during the Weimar period. But the Nazis' mobilization of both industrial and military machines was utterly modern. Francisco Franco's Spain and Salazar's Portugal were more determinedly conservative, only accepting modernization when pressed on them by the technocratic Catholic organization Opus Dei in the late 1950s.

All these movements, like radical Islam today, took politicized pessimistic nostalgia to its logical conclusion of a love of killing. If one is trying to hold on to something existentially threatened when all conflicts must be zero-sum in a shrinking world, one sees extreme contestation for space – both literal and metaphorical – and therefore looks to the physical elimination of rival contenders for that space. The interwar fascists were quite open in their worship of violence. Today, although there is nearly always a physically violent wing to pessimistic movements, they are usually held at the margins by the core leadership, though there remains ambiguity. In Hungary the violent, anti-Jewish, xenophobic Jobbik

(Movement for a Better Hungary) stands to the right of Fidesz, the party of Prime Minister Viktor Orbán, opposes it at elections, and is rejected by it, though there are links between them. The Law and Justice Party in Poland (Prawo i Sprawiedliwość, PiS) has similarly ambiguous relations with extreme nationalist, anti-Jewish groups. In France the *gilets jaunes* (yellow vest) protests against President Macron in 2018–19 achieved levels of violence rarely seen even in France's occasional very open street conflicts. Far-right groups were involved in the protests, but so was the far left, and it was difficult to discern who was steering any of the action. Waves of hate crimes against ethnic minorities followed the UK referendum to leave the EU, the election of Donald Trump as president of the US, both in 2016, and the entry of La Lega into government in Italy in 2018. Trump also famously spoke of the 'very fine people' who participated in (as well as those who opposed) a murderous neo-Nazi rally in Charlottesville in 2017, and of the 'beauty' of barbed wire with reference to the border between the US and Mexico. The US alt.right places particular stress on the right of citizens to bear and use firearms. When, in 2018, British members of parliament seeking an extreme form of Brexit wanted to demonstrate their power against the then prime minister, Theresa May, they chose to do it by sabotaging her government's attempt to follow a police request to ban high-powered rifles.

The only important explicit exponent of political violence against domestic opposition in the contemporary alt.right has been Jair Bolsonaro, elected president of Brazil in 2018. He looks back with open nostalgia to the military dictatorships of the 1960s to 1980s that practised torture and murder of political opponents. It is however notable that three of today's most important alt.right leaders – Orbán, Trump and Matteo Salvini (leader of La Lega and, until August 2019, deputy prime minister of Italy) – have been enthusiastic in their admiration for Bolsonaro. The Brazilian leader embodies every item in the pessimistic nostalgia catalogue: explicit nostalgia for a specified past period, implying also a fondness for violence; Protestant Christian fundamentalism; a deeply traditionalist approach to the role of women; homophobia; the denial of climate change, reflected in his determination to intensify the destruction of the tropical rain forests; and a contempt for ethnic minorities, in his case not immigrants, but the descendants of the aboriginal people of Brazil.

The attack that the alt.right launches against established elites usually includes a demand for direct people power, for the assertion of the expression of the discontents of the people against various institutions that try to restrain them. Since it is not possible for direct democracy to make the complex decisions of modern societies, this demand is always a sleight of hand. There are always leaders whose job it is to interpret, indeed personify, the people's will. This was analysed by Yves Mény and Yves Surel in their 2001 study of populism, when the current resurgence was in its infancy. Similar arguments have been eloquently developed more recently by Jascha Mounk (2018) and Jens-Werner Müller (2018). These movements, they argue, always require a charismatic leader in whom total trust is placed, as the populism they espouse is intolerant of intermediary institutions. The leader claims to speak for, indeed to personify, 'the people'. There is always a definite article here, a singular mass with a settled will, leaving no scope for minorities. Those who do not share the majority view are deemed to be hostile to the people and should have no rights to speak. All intermediate institutions that might stand in the way of or modify the leader's – standing for the people's – will are likewise anti-democratic enemies. The authors cited above see a direct link between the assertion of leaders' power and the strong use that these movements make of hostility to ethnic minorities within and foreign countries without. This hostility binds the unity of the national people, a unity that makes it difficult to quarrel with the leader without being vulnerable to the charge of treason.

Populist leaders of this kind are immune from many of the sources of disillusion confronted by normal political movements, who, when in office, are often unable to fulfil their promises. All that the alt.right offers its supporters is legitimation of the right to hate – an offer that is not vulnerable to inflation or public spending constraints. Time runs out for the alt.right's promises only if and when people start doubting that the objects of their hatred are really the cause of all their dissatisfaction. History does not tell us much about the likelihood of this occurring. The successful xenophobic movements of the interwar years abolished free elections soon after they had consolidated their power.

We can learn more about the directions in which pessimistic nostalgia is taking democracy by briefly examining some of the cases mentioned above in more detail.

The US

The Republican Party of Donald Trump in the US brings together most elements of the alt.right. For decades now, the main divisions in American politics have concerned the country's so-called 'culture wars': conservative approaches to religion, gender and race, enthusiasm for the death penalty and the right of citizens to bear firearms pitting pessimistic nostalgia against various forms of liberalism. The US political right tends to be fundamentalist Christian, the main concern of which is opposition to abortion. This in turn signals an approach to gender that expresses discontent with freedoms and rights that have been won by American women, especially over their bodies – a discontent that is shared by women with generally conservative values, just as it is rejected by many men. The right to bear and use highly sophisticated firearms is a second fundamental component. It is nostalgic, as it harks back to the early days of the American republic (though the firearms that it was then deemed safe for citizens to carry around all day were cumbersome, single-shot muskets, not semiautomatic assault weapons). Concern over arms-bearing is pessimistically violent in its assumption that one is likely to need to defend oneself and one's property with lethal force. The prominence of support for capital punishment on the US right runs along similar lines. The same groups are usually also hostile to evidence that human action has anything to do with climate change. While these views are encouraged by the very wealthy individuals and corporations with major interests in heavily polluting industries who fund US conservatism, climate change denial also suits the mind set of pessimistic nostalgia: the world is probably getting worse; all we can do is defend our immediate interests; why care about the long-term future? Nostalgia can also be seen in the hostility to scientific knowledge of much US conservatism, science being an epitome of modernity. This is eagerly embraced by the opponents of scientific knowledge concerning climate change, but it also includes support for the biblical account of the creation of the universe, and hostility to the use of vaccination to limit the spread of infectious diseases. The last-mentioned, which is embraced by Trump, has also acquired strong support in Italy alongside the rise of the alt.right in that country.

These US movements are overwhelmingly white, race being one of the fault lines dividing the many strands of American politics. Attempts to exclude or 'send home' members of minority races represent one of the most potent forms of pessimistic nostalgia. Trump made an important gesture towards such sentiments in July 2019, when, in a series of tweets, he told four non-white female members of the US Congress that they should go back to their own 'broken and crime-infested' countries, and accused them of supporting Islamic terrorist groups. In fact, only one of the women was born outside the US, but the importance of his remarks was the signal that people from certain ethnic backgrounds were not really US citizens, wherever they were born. If they went away, there would be more space and resources for 'true' Americans. US alt. right movements are also strongly nationalistic, resenting challenges to American global, political, economic and, in particular, military dominance. Another key feature of US neoconservatism is rejection of organizations of international cooperation, seen vividly in Trump's hostility to such bodies as the United Nations, the North Atlantic Treaty Organization (NATO), the EU, and the WTO.

This limb of the US body politic is confronted by one that is broadly definable as liberal. Adherents to liberal culture might be religious, but not necessarily; they will almost certainly be favourable towards gender and racial equality, and internationalist. In recent years, attitudes towards sexual orientation and sexual identity have been added to the cultural confrontation. In the case of each issue, the right stands for clarity of traditional distinctions that it believes are being destroyed, and discourages tolerance of the 'other'. Liberals stand for tolerance and a positive approach to diversity and change. They are, however, strongly divided between neoliberals and egalitarians, the latter resembling the European social democratic left. Since the 1970s, neoliberalism has become the centre of political consensus in the US in a way that did not occur in western Europe until later. This facilitated a very broad liberal consensus, but it also meant that dissatisfaction with the consequences of financial deregulation could be redefined as dissatisfaction with cultural rather than with economic globalization. American neoliberals are themselves divided over these culture wars. For many of them, barriers of the religious, gender, racial and gender kind are just as much obstacles to economic freedom as are progressive taxation and the welfare state, and they therefore do not associate themselves with the conservative cultural crusade. Others see in the cultural issues an opportunity for neoliberal economics to avoid the conservative attack and indeed associate themselves with it, as Nancy MacLean (2018) has shown in her study of the organization of the US right.

Trump represents a compromise between these two, using conservative values to attack immigrants, foreign trade and international organizations, while intensifying the neoliberal deregulation of finance. Although Trump is himself part of America's economic elite, boasts of his wealth and was elected on the platform of a major party, he is also an alt.right outsider, using the mantra that it is the liberal-minded among the US wealthy who have dominated the country, undermined its traditional values and accepted both immigration and the participation of the US in a global order that requires it to compromise. His rise was initially opposed by the Republican establishment (though most of them subsequently threw in their lot with him), and he has demonstrated a typical populist impatience with formal institutions, attacking law courts whose decisions have stood in his way.

It is difficult for west European observers to understand some aspects of American institutions. From the founding of the republic in 1776, the US Constitution has rejected the concept of an established state church. Throughout the nineteenth and early twentieth centuries, this spared the US from the conflicts experienced in many European countries over the role of such churches. Paradoxically, however, it makes it possible for different religions (and agnosticism) to fight to exercise informal influence over national politics. Politicized religious conflict in the US is therefore more important and divisive than anywhere in western Europe. Similarly, the US Constitution set the world an example of the separation of political and judiciary power, and the subordination of the former to a Supreme Court charged with interpretation of the Constitution. Paradoxically, again, this has served only to intensify the importance of the political balance of courts. One can keep courts institutionally separate from governments, but one cannot prevent organized currents of cultural opinion represented by parties from trying to get control of both. This has long been the case. Its effect has been mitigated by the fact that judges serve for life, enabling layers of changing political majority opinion to be represented, and by general polite norms of all sides using criteria of judicial competence rather political attitudes to determine votes on candidates. The latter has now changed radically, with Republicans in particular in recent years using a series of tactics in order to ensure the selection of conservative judges, especially to the Supreme Court.

Central and Eastern Europe

For reasons that we shall examine in the following chapter, voters in central and eastern Europe have found it difficult to establish stable political identities. Parties come and go, often just based around a rich individual. Participation in elections has been falling, despite the initial enthusiasm at the arrival of liberal politics following the fall of state socialism. Many of the countries of the region have important histories of struggle against foreign domination, whether by Russia and the Soviet Union, Germany or the Austro-Hungarian Empire. Nationalist sentiments are therefore strong. In Hungary, Viktor Orbán was the first political leader in the region to realize that conservative nationalism could provide an enduring connection between politicians and the mass public, and he has developed the ideology of twenty-first-century social conservatism more thoroughly than anyone else. He describes his mission as leading an illiberal turn in public values, based on conservative Christianity. As a linguistically distinct country with various longstanding cultural minorities within its borders, Hungary provides fertile soil. Orbán's image of Hungary is that of the country during the Austro-Hungarian Empire, dismembered in 1918, and therefore includes implicit claims to parts of neighbouring countries with large Hungarian minorities. He has gone on to use illiberalism as a justification for subordinating Hungary's law courts to political control. He has also started to restrict academic freedom, initially concentrating his attack on the Central European University in Budapest, which is funded by George Soros, the Hungarian-American billionaire who has funded various organs of liberal thought in Europe and the US. Being Jewish, Soros has become a symbol of the cosmopolitanism that the alt.right detests, the Italian and US right also using his name as a term of abuse. Meanwhile, public contracts are used to reward individuals and firms supporting Orbán's party, Fidesz, and to punish those opposed to it.

Orbán has now been imitated by the PiS in Poland, led by the former prime minister, Jarosław Kaczyński, with a similar appeal to nationalistic conservative Catholic values and attacks on the autonomy of the judiciary. A *casus belli* was provided in these cases, and also in Bulgaria, the Czech and Slovak Republics and Slovenia, by the EU's attempt to persuade the central European countries to help share the burden of refugees landing on the coasts of Greece and Italy – the lack of such a sharing having ironically fuelled the alt.right in Italy.

Resurgent nationalism in central Europe has a paradoxical relationship to Russia and its leader, Vladimir Putin, which itself reflects the complex relationship between today's Russia and the former Soviet Union, and indeed state socialism's own place on the left–right spectrum. The USSR was understandably hated by most central European nationalists; the Polish extreme right in particular regards the EU as being equivalent to the Soviet regime – a trope also used by British Conservatives. On the other hand, Putin is regarded as a highly sympathetic figure by Orbán, as well as by Salvini in Italy. Trump has also made it clear that he is more in sympathy with Putin's Russia than with either the EU or NATO. At Putin's own rallies, banners have depicted him with Trump and Marine Le Pen, the leader of the French Front National (now renamed the Rassemblement National). Pessimistic nostalgia in central Europe ambiguously also takes the form of a longing for a return to the securities of the state socialist system against the uncertainty of the neoliberal economy. East Germans speak of 'Ostalgie', a neologism implying nostalgia for the east (*Ost*). Also, the current

Russian regime associates itself with all the main tenets of social conservatism: nationalism, traditional relations between men and women, intolerance of homosexuality, rough treatment of liberal political opponents, tolerance of violence and a penchant for military display. Russia is also active in funding alt.right movements and parties in Hungary and Italy, and played a major role in funding (largely illegally) both Trump's 2016 election campaign and the campaign to persuade British citizens to vote to leave the EU.

Western Europe

In western Europe, most countries have important socially conservative, xenophobic political parties. Some of these, particularly in Austria and Sweden, have roots leading directly back to Nazism, though their current leaders claim to have changed. In Denmark and Norway, minority coalitions of conservatives and liberals have depended on alt.right parties for parliamentary support, but not as members of the government. Only in Austria, Italy and Switzerland have such parties held office.

The FPÖ is not a new movement, but has been the party of those nostalgic for Austria's Nazi past ever since the foundation of the Second Republic after the Second World War. It remained small until it adopted a new populist, anti-immigrant rhetoric in the 1980s, but then again stagnated until the recent wave of mainly Islamic refugees enabled it to take votes from both the social democrats and, in particular, the main conservative party, the Österreichische Volkspartei (ÖVP). The latter responded by completely reinventing itself also as a xenophobic populist party. The reinvention worked, and in the 2017 parliamentary elections the ÖVP overtook the social democrats as the first party and formed a coalition with the FPÖ; this coalition collapsed in 2019 following scandals within the FPÖ. Although the government adopted various nostalgic positions – including a reversal of the ban on smoking in public places – it concentrated its attention on reducing the rights of immigrants, in particular Islamic ones.

In Switzerland the Schweizerische Volkspartei (SVP) is also not a new movement, descending from a farmers' party founded in the early twentieth century. This was a minor influence in Swiss political life, until the 1990s, when, like the ÖVP 20 years later, it reshaped itself as a xenophobic movement and rapidly became one of the most important parties in the multiparty Swiss system. Early in the present century its more moderate members split off and formed a rival conservative movement; the SVP became more extreme and, following the European refugee crisis, has attracted even more support. It is now the largest party in the Swiss state, concentrating on Europhobia and hostility to immigrants and refugees.

Although the SVP is the largest in Switzerland, it has less than 30 per cent of the vote, and therefore plays only a minority role within the permanent coalitions of Swiss government. Italy is the only western case to date where a new alt.right party has dominated a government. The Lega Nord was founded in the upheaval of the post-war party system in the early 1990s as a northern separatist movement hostile to the southern part of the country, seeking the creation of a new country to be called Padania. It had some modest success, and gradually added hostility to Islamic immigrants to its repertoire. Before the parliamentary elections of 2018, the party dropped 'Nord' from its logo and literature, abandoned its northern separatism and presented itself as a patriotic all-Italy party, concentrating entirely on hostility to Islam and the failure of Italian governments and the EU to cope with the large numbers of refugees. Its leader, Matteo Salvini, has close links to Orbán and they campaign on each other's behalf, even though it has been the latter who has done most to prevent the EU from helping Italy by sharing the arriving immigrants among the other member states. The rest of the Italian right and centre right threw in their lot with La Lega, forming an effective campaigning coalition in the 2018 elections, subsequently forming a short-lived government with M5S.

Both La Lega and M5S are hostile to Italy's membership of the EU, but have had difficulty in articulating this position given the generally strong support of the Italian public for membership. They have had more success in policies reducing the rights of and forms of assistance available to refugees and migrants. La Lega also stimulated a general climate of xenophobia, an important target of which has been the opposition member of parliament and former minister Cécile Kyenge. She was born in the Congo, but has spent most of her life in Italy, practising as an ophthalmologist before becoming entering politics. In 2013, when Kyenge was a government minister, Roberto Calderoli, a Lega member of parliament and later vice-president of the Italian Senate, publicly called her an orang-utan. Following these and similar remarks from Lega figures, Kyenge called the Lega a racist party. For this, Salvini sued her for defamation. Another target of Salvini's hostility was Domenico Lucano, mayor of Riace, a tiny commune in Calabria. Lucano acquired international attention for his highly successful policy of integrating asylum seekers into the local economy and society. He was arrested on a number of charges of aiding illegal immigration and was temporarily banished from entering the town of which he was mayor.

Salvini has also been very critical of the doctrine that the judiciary should be independent of the policies of the government of the day. In June 2019, he asked officials to examine whether magistrates could be prevented from passing verdicts on cases involving immigrants if the magistrates concerned were known to hold views on the migration issue that differed from government policy. The issue was prompted by decisions on separate cases by three female magistrates in Bologna and Florence. The following month a Sicilian judge held that there were no grounds for holding in prison Carola Rackete, captain of a German charitable ship, the *Sea Watch*, which had rescued

40 migrants in the Mediterranean and brought them to shore in the Italian island of Lampedusa. The Lega/M5S government had banned vessels from landing migrants on Italian soil, and Rackete was arrested when she docked her ship. The court however found that there was no criminal offence in bringing a ship carrying migrants to shore. Salvini insisted that it was an outrage for judges to make such decisions when they knew that the government was opposed to the landing of migrant vessels.

The UK and Brexit

In the UK, the decision to leave the EU (so-called 'Brexit') has been an important expression of pessimistic nostalgia. Although it has been officially presented as enabling a 'global Britain' to leave behind the narrow frontiers of Europe, the core of the debate has been about the need to exclude immigrants and reduce cooperation with neighbouring countries – to 'take back control', in the main slogan of the Brexit campaign. But even 'global Britain' is nostalgic, as the only reason for believing that the UK could find a more global destiny than the rest of Europe outside the EU is the fact that it once ruled a major empire, preferring to relate to its colonies than to its neighbours, and it is primarily to the former countries of that empire that the British government looks when seeking trade partners to replace Europe.

The Brexit referendum and its aftermath also laid bare a number of elements of the alt.right's difficulties with constitutions and the relationship of government to law. The issue was made complex by the fact that the UK has no written constitution, and constitutional law – probably uniquely in the democratic world – can be changed by a simple parliamentary majority. The dominant governing concept is that of parliamentary sovereignty. For much of the UK's democratic history, the majoritarian voting system has granted a duopoly to the two major parties, usually able to form a single-party government dominating parliament. This means that parliamentary sovereignty has been virtually synonymous with government sovereignty, which in turn has meant a concentration of de facto sovereignty in the hands of a prime minister. Government has been subject to the rule of law in the sense of not being able to act illegally, but, in the absence of a written constitution, the courts are often unable to decide whether government might have acted against constitutional principles. Government is therefore not subordinate to judicial authority over constitutional matters. Referenda have been used rarely, but within the informal nature of the constitution they have acquired a role, albeit poorly defined. In principle, parliamentary sovereignty means that referenda are only advisory, but in the case of the 2016 referendum on the UK's membership of the EU, parliament resolved that it would accept the referendum result. However, this left ambiguity about the relationship of that particular referendum to British constitutional norms and electoral law.

Following the referendum, the then prime minister, Theresa May, declared that it was her job to interpret its meaning and to bring separation from the EU to fulfilment. This led to a challenge in the courts by plaintiffs arguing that parliament could not be excluded from decisions over the terms of the severance. The supreme court accepted this plea, leading two leading Conservative newspapers, *The Daily Mail* and *The Daily Telegraph*, to speak respectively of the court as 'enemies of the people' and of 'the judges versus the people'. The former phrase was echoed by several government ministers. Government had to accept the court's ruling, but maintained a further position that was beyond the reach of legal appeal. It passed legislation through parliament that initially brought into British law all current legal provisions accepted as part of the country's membership of the EU, but announced that any subsequent derogation from those provisions would be passed as secondary legislation. Following a principle established under the dictatorial sixteenth-century regime of Henry VIII, secondary legislation does not need to pass through parliament. Since EU law covers a very large proportion of public policy, this amounted to the removal from parliamentary scrutiny of much government business. Further debate over Brexit was concerned with what the referendum decision to leave the Union actually meant. Did it require leaving the European single market and the jurisdiction of the ECJ? Norway is a member of both these, but not of the EU as such. Did it include leaving the Customs Union? Turkey is a member of the Customs Union, but not of the EU.

Since protagonists of the Brexit referendum campaign were not a government but a disparate group brought together for the occasion and lacking any formal responsibility for the outcome, it had been possible for some of them to take up different positions. Since the referendum itself had given no clear answer to these questions, the prime minister announced that she would interpret the people's will. She secured an agreement with the EU and its other 27 member states, but was unable to secure parliamentary support for it, different groups arguing over whether the agreement represented the 'will of the people' expressed in the referendum. Arguments that there should be a second referendum to enable citizens to express a view on the terms eventually negotiated were met with the contention that the people had already spoken, and that giving them a second opportunity to do so would be undemocratic. By June 2019, May had resigned, opposed by both those who wanted no compromise with the EU and those who wanted the UK to remain in the organization. It was, however, also clear that there was no majority support in parliament for leaving the EU without any agreement about future relations. This led to open discussion in Conservative circles that a new prime minister might prevent parliament from meeting until a departure from the EU with no agreement had been accomplished, on the grounds that parliament was standing in the way of the people and was therefore undemocratic. At the time of writing, the issue remains unresolved.

The ill-defined nature of British referendum law also facilitated illegality in the Brexit campaign. It has been established that various US billionaires associated with the alt.right (in particular Robert Mercer, discussed in Chapter 2) illegally channelled large sums of money into the Brexit campaign, largely through an IT company, Cambridge Analytica, which illegally acquired details of the preferences and views of millions of British voters and targeted large numbers of social media messages to them. It is equally well established that the government of Russia illegally passed around £8 million to Arron Banks, one of the leaders of the 'unofficial' wing of the Brexit campaign, who also used the money for social media targeting. Well over a billion social media messages were targeted on individuals in this way, using the techniques described in Chapter 2. UK election law imposes fines for illegal spending, and in parliamentary and local government elections successful candidates whose campaigns benefited from such spending usually lose their seats. Fines were imposed on the 'leave' campaigns because of their illegal funding, but the government decided that this had no implications for the outcome of the referendum.

The British case contains several components of the anti-democratic stance of the alt.right: that law courts should have no right to assess the legal soundness of a government's action, and that illegality should not stand in the way of the alt.right's campaigns; that parliament should have no role once the people have spoken; that the people may speak just once, after which a leader interprets their views; that the people are a singular entity, 'the' people, to the extent that even a minority as large as 48 per cent do not constitute real, in the sense of democratically legitimate, people. The alt.right was not successful on many of these points, and constitutional institutions survived most of the attacks. It is however notable how many of the elements of the pessimistic nostalgia agenda have been present in the Brexit issue.

The challenges to constitutional norms raised by Brexit found resonance in public opinion. The 2019 edition of the annual survey of British attitudes to politics conducted by the Hansard Society found that a majority – 55 per cent – would like to be governed by a strong leader 'willing to break the rules', while only 23 per cent opposed such an idea (Hansard Society 2019). A large minority (42 per cent) also preferred government to be able to avoid parliamentary approval of its actions. The survey also found a significant majority (63 per cent) believing that the system was 'rigged to the advantage of the rich and powerful'. What was not clear was whether those holding that belief included most of those seeking a strong, rule-breaking leader. The answer to that question would tell us much about whether awareness of the problems of post-democracy is leading mainly to support for the alt.right.

Conclusion: The Non-Democratic Supports of Democracy

In the following chapter we shall pursue some of the wider implications of the recent emergence of pessimistic nostalgia for the political culture of post-democratic societies. But the discussion has also revealed the anti-democratic tendencies of the alt.right, or xenophobic populism: the insistence that the will of the people should achieve direct expression through its leaders without interference from intermediate institutions; and the flirtation with hatred and violence that almost inevitably accompanies movements that seek the exclusion and rejection of people of whom they disapprove, especially on ethnic grounds, in what they see as a zero-sum struggle. The tendency of the alt.right to break with formal rules and, in particular, to demonstrate impatience with intermediary institutions that check the exercise of democratically elected power further raises the question of the direction in which pessimistic nostalgia is moving, and the core problem of whether its continuity makes the same contribution to democracy as its initial irruption.

This returns us to the issue discussed in previous chapters of the non-democratic supports of democracy. Even when we accept the need for our democratic rights to be expressed through the election of representatives rather than directly, our relationship to those representatives remains problematic. When they take on government roles, they are equipped with power, which they are often tempted to abuse by means that range from simple corruption to the suppression of their opponents. We need parliaments to check the conduct of the executive; we need the subordination of government to an independent judiciary as a check against the illegal use of power and some forms of corruption. The tendency of populist movements, especially those rooted in pessimistic nostalgia, to regard themselves as the perfect and final manifestation of democracy paradoxically renders them as its enemies. Institutions that might have protected the people from betrayal, corruption, manipulation and ultimately repression by the leader are swept away, their apparent interference in the popular will being impatiently scorned. A fundamental problem of the Brexit referendum has been its status as irreversible, a once-and-for-all-time expression of will, so endowed with democratic legitimacy that the people who themselves gave that expression must never be allowed to rethink it; government alone should be permitted to interpret and reinterpret it. Brexit is therefore an example of illiberal democracy, not only because its principal message expressed pessimistic nostalgia, but because of the constitutional innovations it has brought in its wake.

The initial irruption of populist movements of various kinds within a society may well invigorate its democracy, bringing neglected issues to the table and putting established parties and elites on their mettle. However, unless

Politicized Pessimistic Nostalgia

such movements rapidly change their character to accept restraining institutions, their continued presence can threaten democracy. Nevertheless, the deficiencies in democratic institutions revealed by the rise of populism remain. It is essential that rallying calls to oppose it do not lapse into complacency over post-democracy, defences of corruption, of the plutocratic capture of government, of party systems that no longer represent society's most important divisions. Rude invaders must be welcome, provided they accept that they themselves must become subject to constraints that safeguard democracy's future. That itself will partly depend on whether new, or radically reshaped old, parties can engage in genuine two-way communication, not a post-democratic, manipulative, top-down use of social media that pretends to speak for a 'people' defined so vaguely that it can be held to want whatever the leaders decide it wants.

But are post-industrial, post-religious, post-modern societies capable of producing solidly established political identities, or are we now doomed to be masses of loosely attached individuals blown around by confusing blasts? Pessimistic nostalgia is producing an answer to that question: uncompromising rootedness in nation and ethnicity, allied with other forms of social conservatism. Do the left and centre have anything of similar strength to offer, based on deeply felt social identities? In *Post-Democracy* I mentioned three movements that had been still capable of doing this in recent years: feminism, environmentalism and xenophobic populism. I did not anticipate the power of pessimistic nostalgia lying behind the last of these. How inevitable is its domination? This requires, first (in Chapter 6), a closer look at what happened to the political identities forged during the twentieth century, and then (in Chapter 7) an examination of the potentiality of other forces and movements today.

6
The Fate of Twentieth-Century Political Identities

I originally identified two principal causes of post-democracy – neither anybody's fault and neither easily reversed. The first was the globalization of the economy, which removed the most important issues of economic regulation beyond the reach of national politics, the level at which democracy was usually best established. The second was the decline of the social identities of class and religion that had shaped the main party loyalties of twentieth-century democracy. The reasons why globalization would eventually provoke movements rooted in pessimistic nostalgia centred on a revival of nationalism are easy to grasp. The role of the declining power of class and religion is less obvious, but ultimately more important. It will be discussed here.

While it is tempting to attribute politicians' aloofness from other citizens to arrogance and vanity, there are real problems in that relationship that will afflict even those politicians who have the best will in the world. Most people are not highly political and usually feel remote from what goes on in parliaments and local council chambers. To understand a single political issue and work out one's position on it is a highly complex process, requiring considerable information. To engage in the ostensibly simple act of voting requires even greater complexity, as here the rational voter would have to establish a position on a mass of different issues and then rank them in importance. In theory, one's decision to vote for a particular party would result from a calculation that the number and importance of issues where one agreed with the positions of that party were greater than those where one agreed with others. But in fact, a rational voter would do nothing of the kind, as the minimal effect that one's vote can have on an election outcome could not justify the research time and effort that such an activity would require. Although public political debate routinely speaks as though people made these calculations, the idea is entirely unrealistic.

What we really do when we vote – and we do this not because we are idle or unintelligent, but because we are rational – is to identify a party (or a person if the electoral community is small) that seems to stand for the interests and values of people 'like us'. We might reach this judgement through a general impression of the things they represent, combined with the assessments made by people we trust, mainly family and close friends and neighbours. If we feel we are able to identify (with) a party in this way, we are likely to vote for it. This will change if the party does something to lose our trust, or behaves incompetently, or if our own circumstances change so much that we change our idea of 'people like us'. We might then seek out a different party, or just give up voting.

Decades of the stable operation of this process in western Europe, North America, India, Australasia, but not many other places, led even professional commentators to take it for granted that it operated more or less automatically: introduce universal suffrage, and voters will line up behind a couple of major parties and a sprinkling of small ones. But its lack of obviousness was anticipated in 1882 by

Private Willis, a character in Gilbert and Sullivan's comic opera *Iolanthe*, who sang:

> I often think it's comical – Fal, lal, la!
> How Nature always does contrive – Fal, lal, la!
> That every boy and every gal
> That's born into the world alive
> Is either a little Liberal
> Or else a little Conservative!
> Fal, lal, la!

In 1882, only a minority of 'boys' in the UK and no 'gals' at all had the vote. In that country, and elsewhere, there were at that time (and later) major, occasionally violent, struggles over who should be admitted to political citizenship, these struggles usually being focused on social characteristics that would either entitle their bearers to participation or exclude them from it. If one possessed a social identity that entitled one to citizenship (mainly ownership of a certain level of property or adherence to a particular religion), one might logically identify with a political party that promised to protect that entitlement from encroachment from the propertyless classes or followers of deviant faiths. Conversely, if one were a member of an excluded group, one might well support a party seeking to represent it, and following success in achieving the suffrage, continue to support it. What happens with such a process is that a social identity that one knows one has and constitutes part of one's daily experience acquires a political meaning and alignment. The gap between the social and the political that is ordinarily difficult for most people to surmount is bridged.

The Decline of Class and Religion

Nearly all established liberal democracies have party systems based on struggles over these two key issues dating back to the nineteenth and early twentieth centuries. In some cases, there were further cleavages, such as that between urban and rural. Occasionally, principally in the US and Ireland, parties were based on the outcomes of past civil wars, but in all cases battles over exclusion and inclusion were involved. With the exception of these two countries, the main parties that emerged from the process were: conservative and Christian ones, defending traditional values and interests and classes that had long been political insiders; and social democratic, socialist and labour ones, representing class outsiders, mainly the industrial working class, and sometimes either minority faiths or those professing no religion at all. Such a set of alignments left many people with cross-pressured identities – for example, manual workers allied closely to the dominant form of Christianity, or secularized property owners. Sometimes these adhered to smaller parties, or they chose which of their identities was more important to them. Also, because of this cross-pressuring, many major parties ensured they did not cut themselves off entirely from groups to which they might otherwise seem opposed. For example, although Catholic parties in countries where the church was dominant had histories of association with aristocratic and other privileged groups, those countries also developed Catholic labour movements, all such Catholic groups eventually gathering under the umbrella of Christian democracy.

There is a deep paradox about this process whereby masses of ordinary people were able to acquire a political identity. While eventually it made possible an era of stable and peaceful democracy, its origins were in conflicts of extreme rejection of shared political space by rival groups: civil wars, periods of violent fascist dictatorship, communist revolutions that also turned into violent dictatorships, extensive strikes that often involved bloody clashes between police and workers. It was only if and when the antagonists in such conflicts came to see that there was no future in continuing repression and violence, accepted universal adult suffrage and turned their conflicts into electoral ones, that the identities forged in those conflicts changed from being sources of disruption and became instead the pillars on which democracy was built. The cross-pressured nature of many people's identities and consequent need for many parties not to be exclusive helped achieve this. Overall, parties rooted in opposed identities became the representatives of rival interests within a system of overall inclusion, the central links between citizens and democracy.

The timing of these developments varied, the world wars playing a major role in encouraging various social groups to accept that their conflicts must take place within some overall shared national interests. In most of western Europe, all men had acquired the vote by the end of the First World War. However, many aristocratic, church and capitalist elites refused to accept this situation, and through the agency of fascist and Nazi parties were able to root out democracy soon after it was born. It required the defeat of these dictatorships in the Second World War to reconcile those elites to the return of democracy. In the US, white men gradually acquired rights to vote during the latter part of the nineteenth century, but blacks did not fully do so until 1962. In Russia, meanwhile, a communist revolution had shown a similar intolerance of the political inclusion of any except the communist working class, and erected a dictatorship to guarantee that position, the Union of Soviet Socialist Republics (USSR). Communist dictatorships were then extended to those parts of central and eastern Europe occupied by the USSR in the wake of the Second World War. Some of these had only weak histories of democracy, but even stronger cases, such as Czechoslovakia, were removed from liberal democratic history until the fall of the state socialist system in 1990.

There was one extraordinary exception to this process of the transformation of social identities into political ones: gender. Women were excluded, everywhere, from virtually all achievements of political citizenship until after the First World War. This is the purest example of the political exclusion of a clearly defined and easily understood identity, and when women did achieve the vote it was only after struggle. And yet there have been very few examples of women's parties, none of them more than marginal. Until women were included, all parties were, by definition, male parties, and many, though not all of them, fought to keep things that way. Once female suffrage was achieved, these same parties started to appeal to women for their votes, and, despite their past records, did so with considerable success. Although conservative and Christian parties had been the most determined to maintain female exclusion, for many years they succeeded in attracting more female voters than socialist and liberal ones.

We can probably explain the failure of women's parties by the fact that, with the exception of some religious groups, men and women do not form separate communities. This tells us something important about the transmission of social identities into political ones: they need to be rooted in communities, in social groups that interact, confirming members' identities and their implications, including political ones. The greater success of conservative and Christian parties in attracting women tells us something similar. These parties, especially Catholic ones, confirmed and celebrated the primary role of women as mothers and wives in societies where women did not participate in paid employment or did so only in very inferior roles. Socialist and labour parties were mainly concerned with advancing the role of 'breadwinner' men, while both they and liberal parties tended to be non- or even anti-Christian, or to represent religious minorities. This eventually changed. Since the general increase in women's labour market participation from the 1970s onwards, men and women have gradually swapped places politically. In virtually all established democracies, more women than men vote for parties of the left (mainly social democratic or green), while men have become more conservative, perhaps experiencing pessimistic nostalgia at women's 'invasion' of their previous monopolies. We shall later explore some of the reasons for and implications of this. For the present, it is important only to note the role of party affiliation as identity affirming, more perhaps than interest advancing. With time, the original struggles over inclusion and exclusion became a memory of the tribulations of past generations rather than an experienced reality. A weakening of their hold on citizens' loyalties therefore had to be expected. Ironically, the very achievement of universal adult citizenship that had been at the heart of the struggle for democracy weakened the bonds that tied citizens to the democratic process. Then the social structure itself changed. The occupations of industrial society on which the class nature of the struggle for and against the extension of the suffrage had been largely based have been disappearing, and with them the resonances that enabled people to feel that, if they occupied a particular place in the occupational structure, it was fairly clear which party most spoke for them. The growing size of firms has produced extensive hierarchies of salaried managers in the place of individual capitalist owners, few of the former, apart from those at the top, having the clear sense of class position enjoyed by the latter. Large numbers of people in the growing services sectors of economies work in occupations that either did not exist at the time of the struggle over political inclusion or were very small at that time. Few are associated with having played leading roles in those conflicts.

In Europe, religion too has declined in social significance. Numbers attending religious services have gone down almost everywhere, and fewer people identify closely with a particular faith. Further, most forms of European Christianity have abandoned the strongly conservative positions that once characterized them. A major development in this respect was the modernizing impetus of the Second Vatican Council of Pope John XXIII in 1962. The church's final conservative struggles have been over various issues relating to family life and gender, as governments legitimated contraception, divorce, abortion, homosexuality and, most recently, bi- and trans-sexuality.

Centre-right parties conceded defeat to the rationalist, secular and scientific ideas of the liberalism that had been their main opponents throughout the nineteenth century. But this did not mean that conservative parties lost out to liberal ones; rather the opposite took place. Liberalism always had a problem appealing to mass electorates. Its very ideology of opposing the barriers forged by strong identities almost prevented it from developing strong cultural roots. When it did have them, it was because they attracted various cultural or religious minorities who sought protection from parties based on majority identities. Conservative and Christian democratic parties, on the other hand, managed to retain the support of people with strong socially conservative values – they had no other home to go to – while adopting those liberal positions that accorded with their role as representatives of the economically successful and many of those aspiring to be such. Liberalism as a political movement was reduced to small minority status almost everywhere, despite the victory of its cultural and economic ideas.

Many, probably most, people in contemporary established democracies no longer have strong social clues to indicate a political identity for them. The weakening of ties between citizens and parties that has been clearly evident in declines in electoral participation and party memberships is widely attributed to disillusion with governments' performances and a sense of betrayal of trust by politicians who have engaged so long in compromises that it is difficult to identify what, or whom, they represent. Whether contemporary politicians are in reality less trustworthy and more corrupt than those of the past is difficult to determine. A perceived decline in trustworthiness may well be merely the consequences of our knowing more about them than in the past, thanks to changing norms of transparency and greater media exposure. But these changing norms are themselves a response to declining levels of trust among citizens, itself in turn a result of a growing distance between them and political leaders. It is entirely possible that there was at least as much deception among politicians of earlier generations as now, but that the closer bonds they enjoyed with their voters prevented the latter from entertaining the possibility.

As class and religion failed to deliver voters as in the past, parties began to look beyond their core constituencies to maximize their votes. Some rejected the very concept of a core, ostentatiously dissociating themselves from the declining constituencies of their past, seeking to become 'catch-all' parties. While this might broaden appeal, it is quite likely further to weaken the strength of a party's ties. Fewer voters could say: 'That is the party that is clearly for people like me (rather than for others).' That process of loosening has been fundamental to post-democratic trends, leading politicians to relate to voters through mechanisms and techniques that resemble commercial advertising campaigns rather than engaging in exchanges with supporters.

We see this change in the declining attraction to voters of the Christian democratic or conservative and social democratic parties that dominated the second half of the twentieth century in western Europe. Figure 6.1 compares the proportion of electorates voting for a country's main centre-right party in parliamentary elections held around 1985 with the most recent elections by mid-2019. Figure 6.2 does the same for the main centre-left party. I am using proportions of total electorates voting for parties rather than proportions of those voting, because declining turnout itself constitutes part of what we understand by declining ties between parties and voters. Particular circumstances may affect a party's position at one election, from which it shoots up or down at a subsequent one; my data here cannot captures such possibilities. However, such major swings, which happen more today than in earlier decades, are themselves evidence of loosening ties between parties and voters.

Figure 6.1 shows a decline for all dominant (or once dominant) centre-right parties except for France and

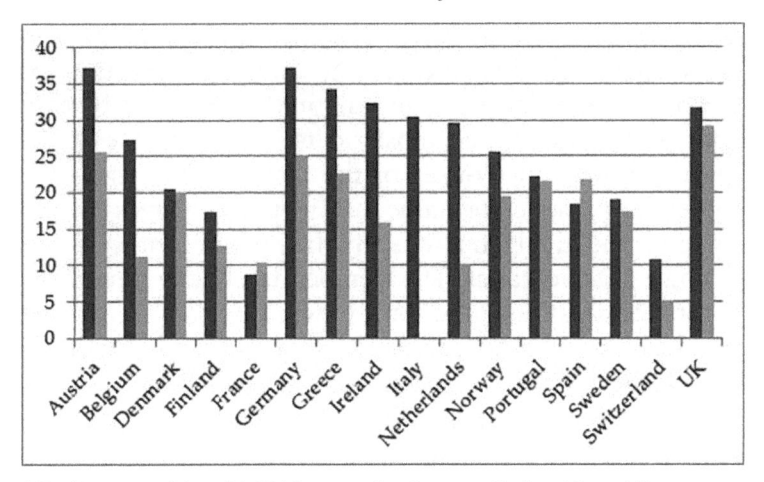

[Bar chart showing percentages from 0 to 40 across countries: Austria, Belgium, Denmark, Finland, France, Germany, Greece, Ireland, Italy, Netherlands, Norway, Portugal, Spain, Sweden, Switzerland, UK]

NB: 'Germany' in mid-1980s was the German Federal Republic; today it is united Germany. Statistics for Belgium add the votes of the separate Flemish and Walloon parties

Figure 6.1 Percentage of electorate voting for main centre-right party, mid-1980s (dark grey) and late 2010s (light grey), west European countries

Source: Author's calculations based on Wikipedia data

Spain, the former being in any case already very small. In Italy, the once commanding Christian Democratic Party collapsed in the early 1990s. Important strands of it continued, moving to both right and left, but by the 2018 elections all the former had been absorbed into a coalition of parties led by La Lega. Italy currently lacks a centre right. Very few of these parties today attract more than a third of the electorate. (The statistic for the UK is misleading, as the country's voting system punishes all minor parties other than those based on a territorial identity, pressing voters to retain support for historically dominant parties.)

Figure 6.2 shows similar declines for all main centre-left parties except for Portugal and the UK, though in the latter case the homogenizing pressures of the electoral system must again be noted. Some collapses have been very dramatic, especially France, Greece and the Netherlands. I have taken the Communist Party to be the main centre-left party in Italy in the 1980s, as by then that party had severed most of its links with the Soviet Union and was no longer of the far left. The party then underwent a series of name and identity changes as well as splits and amalgamations. By the present century it had become I Democratici (The Democrats). By the time of the most recent national elections, previously major centre-left parties were attracting more than a quarter of electorates only in Belgium, Sweden and the UK, and in the first case that is achieved only by adding the votes of the separate Flemish and Walloon socialist parties.

While both political families have been deeply affected, the decline in the stable identities of the twentieth century has hurt social democratic parties more than Christian

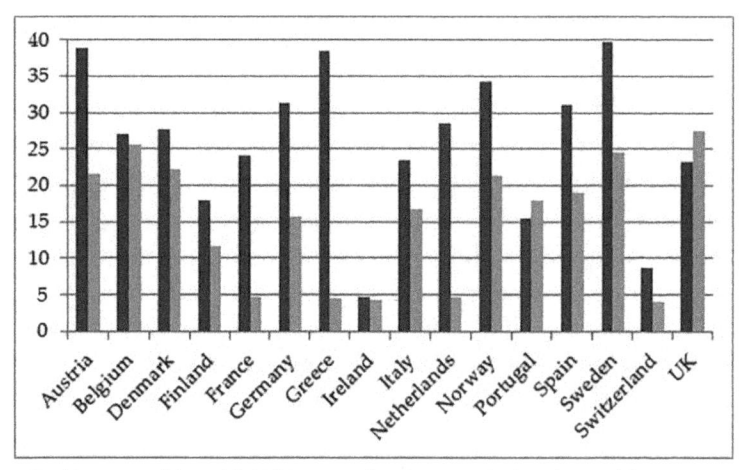

NB: 'Germany' in mid-1980s was the German Federal Republic; today it is united Germany. Statistics for Belgium add the votes of the separate Flemish and Walloon parties

Figure 6.2 *Percentage of electorate voting for main centre-left party, mid-1980s (dark grey) and late 2010s (light grey), west European countries*

Source: Author's calculations based on Wikipedia data

and conservative ones. This may be explained by an important asymmetry in the appeal of the two groups of parties. Party identity can serve as a form of personal identity confirmation: I am of identity X, and therefore I vote for party A. This works unambiguously for identities that people are proud to have, but not so well for those associated with subordination and misery of various kinds, and it is the historic role of parties of the left disproportionately to represent the latter. Arthur Scargill, leader of the British National Union of Mineworkers, who led his once large union into the strike of 1984–5 that marked the last great conflict of industrial Britain, declared that he wanted to secure work in the pits for miners, their sons and their grandsons. This was his (highly gendered) vision of the purpose of socialism. A central aim for many others on the political left, however, was to create a society in which it would no longer be necessary for men to crawl on their bellies in dangerous conditions underground. Social democracy and socialism have been partly identity-confirming forms of politics for working-class people, but they have also sought means of releasing people from those very identities. When people achieve release, they might continue to see their interests as represented by the political left, but they might take as a mark of their social progress that they can now realistically associate themselves with a more conservative form of politics.

The US is an exception to much of this primarily west European story. In Europe, ideas of class in industrial capitalism built on those of social hierarchy of pre-industrial society. Lacking such a past, US industrial class relations did not have that kind of clarity, even though industrial conflict and labour-management relations were often violent. Further, American industrialization was accompanied by massive waves of immigration, immigrants often associating with the cultural and religious groups of their countries of origin. These, and the conflicts of inclusion and exclusion that raged around them rather than class, conferred social identities that could be converted into political ones. There was no state religion, which meant that there could be no formal conflicts around relationship to an established church. Instead, within the extraordinary diversity of beliefs found within American Christianity, Judaism and later other faiths, religious conflicts were converted into cultural ones among groups with different immigrant heritages. A particular set of religious beliefs would become the badge of a wider cultural identity. This is why the US has taken the lead in the politics of culture wars, discussed in the previous chapter, which now affects most of Europe and many other parts of the world.

As Americans became divided over their attitudes to various aspects of modernity, their differences often took religious expression, which renders them particularly profound, as they go beyond the concerns of this world. Overarching all these struggles has been that over race, focused on those in the black population who had been slaves, over whose liberation the Civil War had been fought but who continued to occupy a both socially and politically excluded position in the former slave states of the south.

Despite the complexity of these essentially ethnic cultural divisions, the US electoral system virtually forces all voters into one of two camps, Democrat or Republican, which necessarily become not only catch-all parties, but internally incoherent. The Republicans, the party of Abraham Lincoln, were originally the party of northern liberal capitalism, the enemies of and victors over the slave states of the south. In the south, their liberalism was the more salient; in the north, their position was as the party of an exclusive ruling elite. The Democrats were the party of slavery and, after the Civil War, of the continued suppression of the black population in the south. But they were, as representatives of the defeated, the party of the excluded. In the north, they therefore became the main party of choice for successive waves of immigrants into the northern cities, the new outsiders of industrial America. These contradictions did not begin to resolve themselves until the 1960s, when Democratic presidents Kennedy and Johnson took up the cause of black people. Very gradually, liberal opinion throughout the country, north and south, congregated around the Democratic Party, conservatives around the Republicans. In particular, various brands of Protestant Christianity were available to many mainstream Americans as a symbol of their association with conservative values and therefore a rallying point for the Republicans. The Democrats have been more likely to attract followers of outsider faiths – especially black Protestant churches, Catholics and Jews – or those of no religion, or who did not believe that religion had strong public policy implications. In the 1950s Americans would shake their heads at the deep ideological conflicts over class and religion found in most of western Europe. US party politics, with weak ideas of class and no conflicts over established religion, was, by contrast, free of ideology almost to the point of meaninglessness. This historical pattern has been completely reversed, as US religion has become the focus for increasingly bitter culture wars over race, sexual behaviour and gender. These wars have articulated the confrontation between pessimistic nostalgia and various concepts of modernity that have now spread to include both western and eastern Europe.

From the late 1980s the Democratic Party, which had in any case never been fully social democratic, took on some of the policy approaches of neoliberalism and sought to move away from its declining base among workers in the manufacturing industry and mining. It was followed very soon afterwards by the British Labour Party, and more slowly by other European social democrats. This led these parties to turn their attention away from inequalities based on class and economic issues. Campaigns for reducing inequalities concentrated instead on gender, race and sexual identity. This was quite compatible with neoliberalism, which is opposed to noneconomic forms of inequality. It also matched the parties' search for new constituencies, while partly staying true to their role as representative of various excluded and underprivileged groups. This formula produced a coherent new politics, but at the expense of traditional Democratic, Labour and social democratic constituencies in the declining manual working class, leaving many of the latter receptive to messages of pessimistic nostalgia.

Cultural and Economic Politics

As Private Willis's implicit irony hints, it is not 'Nature' that contrives to impart a stable two-party identity to each new generation of citizens, but the residues of particular histories, which will change over time. Fifty years after his song, the Liberals had been replaced by Labour in the greatly expanded electorate of the UK. Since then, the decline of class and religion has weakened powerful political commitments among early twenty-first-century populations, but politics, like nature, abhors a vacuum. The bearers of political projects logically do what they can to exploit the resources liberated by this decline. Some, primarily environmental and green movements, appeal to a post-identity politics, seeking to mobilize citizens over concerns for the planet itself rather than as social groups struggling over inclusion and exclusion. They bear the same weakness as historical liberalism, seeking a politics that is above identity, and therefore probably doomed to play a minority, if important, role.

I have discussed elsewhere (Crouch 2018) how, since the French Revolution, there have been two principal axes of political conflict: that between conservative traditionalism and liberal rationalism; and that between forces defending economic inequality and those seeking to erode it. The latter was, in practice, a conflict within the liberal bloc, between advocates of, respectively, the liberal market economy and egalitarian social citizenship. During the course of the second half of the twentieth century, conflicts over the first axis gradually declined, though they

The Fate of Twentieth-Century Political Identities 133

remained important, especially in predominantly Catholic countries, for issues of family, gender and sexuality. In general, as democracy became well established and winning the votes of manual workers became central to political success, the second axis, rooted in class conflicts, came to dominate. Political conflict concentrated mainly on issues of redistributive taxation and the size and scope of the welfare state.

Changes in contemporary societies are bringing a return to prominence of the first axis, with traditional conservatism reappearing in its guise of representing pessimistic nostalgia, defending apparently threatened national and religious cultures and gender relations against the disturbing changes of a liberal internationalism. The alliance between conservatives and liberals that had been fairly easy to achieve when second-axis issues of redistribution dominated is becoming fraught. On the other side, although social democracy has always preached internationalism and universalism, in practice the universalism of its welfare states had been limited to the oxymoron of a national universe; and its core social supports had been industrial working-class communities. Increasingly some members of those communities, or what was left of them after globalization and automation, perhaps feeling neglected after social democracy began its flirtation with neoliberalism, have been drawn to pessimistic nostalgia and a conservative nationalism. Meanwhile, social democracy's newer recruits among middle-class professionals have allied with cosmopolitan liberalism. We have arrived at a complex intersection of the two axes, playing havoc with familiar party alignments.

The Swiss sociologist Daniel Oesch was the first to notice these axial changes, in a series of publications in the early years of this century (Oesch 2006a, 2006b; Oesch and Rodríguez Menés 2011). His main concern was dissatisfaction with the idea of an undifferentiated middle class, given that the category was coming to encompass the broad majority of occupational positions in the advanced economies. He proposed that social and political attitudes were formed not just by the positions people occupied in organizational hierarchies (class, relevant to values on the second axis), but by the kinds of work tasks or orientations on which they were engaged (affecting the conservative–liberal axis). He distinguished three kinds of tasks:

1 *Technical*: in a hierarchy of technical experts, technicians, skilled craft workers, routine industrial and agricultural workers.
2 *Organizational*: in a hierarchy of higher-grade managers, associate managers, skilled office workers, routine office workers.
3 *Interpersonal*: in a hierarchy of sociocultural professional workers, sociocultural semi-professional workers, skilled service workers, and routine service workers.

Oesch's research concentrated on Germany, Spain, Sweden, Switzerland and the UK, but his ideas were later applied to all western member states of the EU on issues of direct relevance to us here by two German political scientists working in the US, Herbert Kitschelt and Philipp Rehm (2014). Together, these studies suggest that people engaged on organizational tasks were most likely to have authoritarian attitudes, while those on interpersonal ones were most likely to liberal-minded. Particularly interesting is the fact that Kitschelt and Rehm started with three axes: attitudes to redistribution; authoritarian or liberal values on social behaviour; and more or less inclusive attitudes on citizenship and immigration. However, the latter two tended to collapse into one position corresponding to our first axis: people who believed that immigration should be restricted were also likely to believe that school discipline should be tougher – a classic conservative position.

National identity lies at the heart of concerns about immigration; it is a social identity that people have long been encouraged to feel strongly; and it has political implications. For a long time after the defeat of fascism in the Second World War, mainstream politicians were careful not to exploit the dangerous possibilities of these. This has changed. Major movements of migrants and refugees, with the added frisson of occasional acts of Islamic terrorism, have raised the salience of appeals to apparently threatened national identities. If one adds to this the feelings of loss of national control facilitated by globalization, the rise of xenophobia as a major political force and as the main mobilizing force behind pessimistic nostalgia presents no mysteries of understanding.

Setting the growing importance of nation against the declining salience of class and (in Europe) religion may also enable us to explain some otherwise puzzling features of the present situation. The advanced north European welfare states – the Nordic countries as well as the Netherlands and Austria – all have major xenophobic populist movements, despite their wealth, low levels of social insecurity and of inequality. (Germany is a different and more complex case, because of its particular history of racist politics and its recent unification with a former communist state.) Portugal and Spain – relatively poor (especially Portugal), with less developed welfare states, high levels of inequality, recent victims of imposed austerity policies following the Eurozone crisis – have lacked such movements until, in 2018, some extreme rightist groups in Spain saw the potential of the arrival of refugees from North Africa. Ireland, wealthy but another Eurozone victim of austerity, is also free of xenophobic politics, while Greece, the country that experienced the debt crisis most intensely of all, has only a small xenophobic movement. In southern Europe, only Italy has developed a powerful xenophobic right. It is possible to explain the paradox if one recalls that Greece, Portugal and Spain were not liberal democracies until the 1970s, three decades later than the rest of western Europe. Portugal and Spain, in particular, had experienced long-term rule by conservative dictatorships under which class and religious conflicts had been particularly severe. The hypothesis that political identities based on struggles over inclusion around class and religion 'wear out' over time should lead us to predict that these identities should be holding up better on the Iberian peninsula than elsewhere in western Europe.

How does one then explain the particular virulence of xenophobia in central and eastern Europe, where liberal democracy is even younger, barely a quarter of a century old? Here one must remember the inversion of class struggle that had occurred under state socialism. The working class was deemed to be the leading class, but in reality there was no political citizenship for anyone outside a tiny elite of *nomenklatura*. Universal inclusion was universal exclusion. As noted in the previous chapter, it has been difficult for people in that part of the world to relate to political structures familiar in the west. For a few years after 1990, it seemed that something like Christian and social democratic parties might become the basis of party systems, but these movements fragmented. There was instead a plethora of small, transient parties, with an occasionally larger movement based on a rich individual and his client groups. Meanwhile, all the formal institutions of democracy were in place. Democracy seemed very rapidly to become post-democracy. First Viktor Orbán, then politicians in most of the rest of the region saw the potential of a reawakened nationalism.

Across large parts of the world nationalism is emerging as a force that can enable important numbers of contemporary citizens to relate to the political world. This seems to mark a victory of the first, cultural, axis, over the second, material, one. If so, it represents a momentous change in the history of democracy during the twentieth century. Critics of this viewpoint on the socialist left will point to the role of the 'left behind' in movements of pessimistic nostalgia, implying that material issues lie behind the ostensible cultural turn. However, as was argued in the previous chapter, being left behind economically has been by no means the sole motivating force of this new politics. People living in declining cities and losing their jobs in declining industries constitute small minorities. It is only when they are joined by persons who see themselves as being left behind in other respects, and in particular who attribute this to the presence of cultural and ethnic minorities, that they constitute major movements. If the issues were solely economic, the populist left would have far greater success in mobilizing discontent than an alt. right that in general does not concern itself with economic inequality. The US Republicans, La Lega and Brexit Conservatives also pursue fiscal policies that favour the wealthy. In Hungary, Fidesz is dismantling many labour rights and social policies. The appeal to the poor of the alt.right is that material issues are not as important as cultural ones.

People on the liberal left have spent much of the past two or three decades feeling mainly on the losing side in a struggle with neoliberalism over economic issues, the welfare state and labour rights. They did not notice that on cultural questions they had been on the winning side since the 1960s – often in tacit coalition with neoliberalism. On such matters as gender and sexuality, multiculturalism and relations between countries, on the role of religion in social life and on attitudes to violence, liberal values achieved many victories. Even religious, military and other authorities generally regarded as conservative became increasingly liberal.

A large minority of people was uncomfortable with at least some of these developments. They either believed strongly in conservative values or did not feel confident that they could cope with disorienting changes and sought the reassurance of familiarity. They have felt a burning resentment that very few voices in public life have spoken for them. Because the stern, rather intolerant values that social conservatives hold can easily run to violence if they are stirred up, most established political parties to right, left and centre avoided association with them. Resentment intensified, like floodwater building up behind a dam.

The dam was the basic guarantee of economic and social security that liberal societies continued to offer their citizens. Social conservatives might have felt dissatisfied, but things were not so bad that they wanted to take any serious action. This changed during the first two decades of the new century. Incidents of Islamic terrorism, rare though they may be, together with the financial crisis of 2008 and its aftermath of austerity, made contemporary society seem very much less secure. The dam of liberal society's guarantee had burst.

Issues relating to both axes, the economic and the cultural, worked together to undermine the liberal dam. While neoliberalism partly played a role in weakening the social supports of poor people, it operated far more widely by producing the financial crash of 2008 that made even quite prosperous people feel insecure and therefore hostile to sharing their precious space. Rather than a triumph of the cultural over the economic, recent changes have brought a new configuration of the two. What are the wider implications of this for democracy?

7
Beyond Post-Democracy?

Over recent decades, first neoliberalism and then politicized pessimistic nostalgia have dominated public life. Social democracy, left socialism, (non-neo)liberalism and moderate conservatism have been pushed into corners or have tried to ape either or both of these new arrivals. Neither neoliberalism nor pessimistic nostalgia is in itself anti-democratic; they are both legitimate expressions of political values and interests. However, they both embody threats to democracy if their advocates behave in certain ways, and if their opponents are not alert to these dangers. Interestingly, these threats are of opposite kinds.

I argued in earlier chapters that a strong democracy required two characteristics: a capacity for citizens to confront established elites with unsettling demands; and institutions outside democracy itself that protect its operation, particularly from the conduct of rulers. Neoliberal elites seek to insulate themselves against the former, but are strong in defence of stabilizing institutions that restrict the power of rulers. In fact, they espouse post-democracy: formally adequate institutions that carry out a basic role but have been drained of their democratic vigour. Alt.right movements, in contrast, espouse the unchallenged expression of populist rage, and are therefore impatient with institutions that restrain that expression or, more accurately, restrain the leaders of it. Neoliberals become a danger to democracy when they seek to minimalize the democratic content of protective institutions. The alt.right is a danger when it seeks the liberation of rulers from those institutions.

It was shown in Chapters 2, 3 and 4 that, as neoliberalism became totally dominant over the political economies of the advanced world, the preferences for heavily constrained democracy of its theorists, from Friedrich von Hayek onwards, became clear. The ghost of Hayek and his intense suspicion of democracy were perceived by several observers in the treatment of Greece and Italy during the European debt crisis. Not only were national governments overridden and, in two cases, actually changed, but a specifically ideologically neoliberal interpretation of how national accounts could be stabilized was imposed where this was not the only feasible alternative.

An even larger assault on democracy from neoliberalism had been the earlier liberalization of financial markets, itself one of the main causes of the euro's instability. By enabling these markets to operate with virtually no democratically accountable supervision, deregulation realized neoliberals' dream of the key sector of the economy moving beyond the reach of a democracy that remained restricted to the nation-state. This then had implications across national governments' powers over fiscal, social and many other heartland policy areas. Such a smothering of effective democracy could take place because of the difficulty of extending democratic institutions beyond the nation-state, and the conversion of virtually all major political parties to support some version of the deregulation model. This had in turn been made possible by the weakening of true popular pressure on politicians, who sought their primary associations with the business elite – in other words, by the existing trends towards post-democracy, which then became self-reinforcing.

Neoliberalism has also weakened democracy by undermining the place of values in political debate. It taught generations of politicians that people are motivated by narrow material interests alone and need only be appealed to as though they were customers buying products. There were no collective goods, no public values. Also, one of the main boasts of neoliberal thinkers is that they are able to reduce most decisions to calculations of costs. Since no one can rationally want to waste resources, they argue, we all have an interest in the maximization of efficiency; therefore, when faced with choices we should all rationally choose the most cost-efficient actions. All choices therefore become technical ones. This immediately limits the role of political choice, which is about values and goals, and not purely technical. But, as Laura Pennacchi (2018) has recently convincingly argued, it is not possible to eliminate discussions of values from public life in the way that neoliberalism seeks. The pursuit of efficiency can only be about means; it cannot choose for us the ends for which we are trying to be efficient.

There have been distinctly Pyrrhic elements to neoliberalism's continuing victory in economic policy. First, as discussed in Chapter 2, that very relationship of intimacy between political and business elites that followed its domination undermined its own fundamental tenet that the polity and the economy should be kept separate. That rule came to be a semi-permeable membrane: governments abstained from intervention in the market economy, while businesses lobbied governments for many kinds of favour, from regulatory changes to downright corruption. Many of neoliberalism's favourite policies – such as privatization, public–private financial initiatives, heavily leveraged secondary stock markets, the maximization of shareholder value as the sole goal of a company, deteriorating welfare states – have become disasters. The intensified inequalities produced by financialization and by the declining power of trade unions led to widespread recourse to household debt by medium- and low-income families trying to sustain their consumption levels – levels that capitalism needed in order to sustain its own profits. The financial crisis itself was one of the main consequences of this process. Further, international economic institutions such as the IMF and OECD came to see that growing inequality was threatening the viability of the economic system itself, mainly in the neoliberal heartland of the US, but also more generally. Furthermore, close relations between government officials and business elites remote from democratic scrutiny produced corruption in the awarding of contracts and the influencing of political decisions.

Second, the backlash against neoliberalism eventually fed into the politicized pessimistic nostalgia that has had the neoliberal project of globalization as one of its antagonists. At one level, a return of protectionism in the advanced world would mark a major setback for the neoliberal project. On the other hand, the relationship between these two powerful forces is ambiguous. This can be seen very clearly in the economic policies of the Trump administration. At one level, its planned return to protectionism threatens global free trade. At another, the same administration has reversed the attempts at re-regulation of global finance initiated by President Obama. Trumpite protectionism leaves neoliberalism's most potent and antidemocratic device – unregulated global finance – free of control. The financial markets therefore continue to be able, through the continuing dominance of the also unreformed shareholder maximization model, to nullify national economic policies. The mining and manufacturing industries that Trump claims to be protecting remain vulnerable to these forces. In effect, the alt.right offers neoliberalism a deal: accept nationalistic restrictions on some of your activities, and the rest will be left free. Furthermore, the public's rage will be directed away from

Beyond Post-Democracy? 143

you and on to immigrants and foreigners. Such an offer leaves the neoliberal business world divided, as the alt. right threatens to introduce not only nationalist economic policies, but also to unleash an uncontrolled, anti-institutional political leadership, which is deeply problematic for business interests.

For its own part, pessimistic nostalgia has successfully challenged the enervating value freedom of neoliberal politics. A striking feature of the Europe debate in the UK was the response of the advocates of Brexit to arguments that the economy would be threatened by such a drastic change in the country's economic relationships. It is not only material interests that are at stake, they argued; it might be better to face some decline in living standards in order to protect national culture and values from dilution by immigrants and to avoid a need to cooperate with neighbouring countries. Pessimistic nostalgia encourages the holders of various values who believe themselves to have been neglected for years to express themselves. If these feelings are deeply felt, a strong democracy must enable their expression.

The threat to democracy from the alt.right comes not from the content of its values and ideas as such, but from the attack on the institutions that protect democracy to which they are likely to lead. This threat comes in three forms. First, because the leaders of populist movements are certain that they are right, they are at best heedless and at worst contemptuous of those institutions that limit the risks that leaders will exploit their power. Second, since most of the impetus of these movements stems from resentment at the advances of various, usually not very powerful, groups of people, they are inclined to make use of and stir up hatred. At its worst, this leads to actual physical violence; at best, it contributes to further contempt for restraining institutions, which are seen as serving the interests of hated groups. (The same point applies to left-wing political movements that use hatred of the wealthy as people rather than develop criticism of systems that produce inequality. Such movements become equally contemptuous of restraining institutions.)

Third is the way in which the alt.right uses social media. At one level, these technologies are providing extraordinary opportunities for mobilizing new causes, raising issues and bringing transparency to topics that those in power in governments and corporations would prefer to keep concealed. At another level, we now know what great private wealth, and, at least in the case of Russia, state power, can do to capture, manipulate and distort the role of social media as a genuine form of communication among citizens. We also know that it is the forces of pessimistic nostalgia that are most favoured, often cynically, by wealthy individuals and groups.

Modern societies possess far more extensive resources of knowledge than their predecessors; we use this knowledge to improve our lives to achieve very high standards, and we are dependent on it. But, partly for technical reasons, partly for political ones stemming from the hegemony of neoliberal ideas and corporate wealth, it is increasingly easy for wealthy interests to privatize ownership and control of knowledge – from securing monopoly rights over it to its illegal corruption – and to persuade public authorities to assist the former and turn a blind eye to the latter. In this way our dependence on knowledge becomes a dependence on wealthy interests, the ethics of whose behaviour are only as good as a highly imperfect market requires them to be.

Control over new forms of communication is supplemented by the alt.right's attacks on forms of knowledge that lay beyond their control, mainly professional journalism and science, many of whose practitioners are invulnerable to corruption. The aim is to leave citizens not knowing how to check on the claims that are being made to them through manipulated social media. Donald Trump's famous use of the phrase 'fake news!' to discredit any information hostile to his interests is an example of this, as is his publicity staff's invention of 'alternative facts' to make the news fit his interpretations of what is occurring. Rejection of scientific knowledge reverberates across the US political right, from religious creationists, to climate change deniers, to the anti-vaccination movement, and forms part of the demagogic rhetoric of many kinds of populists reassuring people that important decisions do not require any knowledge, because experts are sometimes wrong. Taken together, these developments are creating a bewildering environment in which it becomes difficult to know what is being communicated, how we can verify it, and who is controlling it.

Of course, politicians who have nothing to do with the alt.right have often lied, distorted evidence and corrupted official statistics to suit their purposes. What is new is the attempt to deny the possibility of neutral knowledge and the idea of evidence itself, an attitude summed up succinctly in the statement in August 2018 by Trump's legal advisor and former mayor of New York, Rudy Giuliani, that 'Truth isn't truth'. It seems strange that large numbers of people in an advanced society like the US have come to be contemptuous of science and knowledge. To understand it, one needs to look at what has been happening for several years to commercial advertising for products; one must remember that commercial advertising is today the main model used for political communications. Modern advertisements, especially on television, rarely give factual information about the products concerned. Instead, they associate them with images and feelings to which the public is likely to respond positively. The idea is that these feelings will then be transferred to the product concerned, even though the images are quite unrelated. So accustomed are we to this technique that very few people regard it as a form of dishonesty. The advertisers do not even claim that there is a factual connection between images, feelings and products. Factual claims have nothing to do with it. We are in a world of post-truth. It is not surprising that politicians have learned to do the same.

An example can be taken from the 2016 EU referendum in Britain. During the campaign, a murder took place in the US, in Orlando, Florida. An American youth, whose parents had come from Afghanistan, had killed 49 people. The anti-EU group Leave.EU quickly produced a short video, which asserted that, if the UK did not leave the EU, such things would happen in England. Using the message multiplication techniques that we have discussed, the campaign was able to achieve many millions of viewings of the video. If one asks what a murder in the US had to do with the EU, particularly when the Islamic minority in the UK does not come from European immigrants but from the British Commonwealth, one does not understand the post-truth world of modern advertising – commercial and political alike. There is no logic of facts and evidence here, but the logic of emotional association. In this particular case, that logic works as follows: Islamists are dangerous and foreign; Europe is full of foreigners; if we want to stay healthy and safe, we should erect strict barriers against foreigners of all kinds. Once a fertile climate has been created no knowledge, argument or reasoning can address that logic.

The super-rich are funding IT tools that enable them to send millions of social media messages, as though from masses of ordinary people but in reality emanating from a single source, transferring into politics the latest commercial advertising techniques. A post-democratic enervation of civil society, powered by post-truth, is posing as its resurgence.

The Dependence of Democracy on Non-Democratic Institutions

At several points in previous chapters I have pointed to democracy's dependence for its own existence and vitality on institutions that are not themselves democratic. My argument here might seem to resemble Hayek's advocacy of constraints placed on the expression of democracy to ensure that it does not interfere with the market. But my concern is not with the protection of markets from democracy, but with the protection of democracy from those who, while democratically elected, have incentives to abuse their mandate. Democracy requires openness and an absence of manipulation, measures to prevent the abuse of power, and mechanisms that ensure continuing debate and opportunities to revise and change opinions. Elected rulers have obvious incentives to abuse and distort all these requirements. They may be prevented from doing so by personal integrity, and this is not a value to be cynically despised. But we cannot rely on it, and therefore need institutions that will protect us from abuse. Although we need democracy to establish these, they then have to be removed from easy meddling by those we have elected. Inevitably, politicians would sometimes like to persuade us that, since they are the embodiment of our democratic will, any institution that hampers their activities is an affront to that will. It then becomes essential that groups and movements that understand the importance of such institutions cry foul and campaign with utmost vigour to point out the abuse that is taking place.

Independent law courts and the subordination of government to the rule of law are the most fundamental and historically best established and understood of these institutions. It is therefore disturbing that so many alt. right movements have targeted autonomous judges as enemies of the popular will because they have reached decisions that populists have found inconvenient. We see this in the constitutional attacks on the independence of the judiciary in Hungary and Poland, in threatening speeches by, for example, Trump, Salvini and the protagonists of Brexit, and on the left in major interferences with judicial independence in Venezuela and elsewhere in Latin America. In a longer historical perspective it was the revolutionary left that challenged the judiciary, which was seen as representative of a ruling class. Conservatives drew much of their prestige from their role as guardians of the constitution. Today, attacks on the judiciary are also coming from the right, and in Europe it has been the social democratic and liberal left that has taken the role of constitutional defence.

The left has also historically been more likely to criticize the independence of central banks as anti-democratic, but some alt.right leaders have joined these criticisms. Certainly, central bank independence was an achievement of 1990s neoliberal reform, and it is consistent with the Hayekian agenda of limiting governments' ability to interfere with the market. By setting interest rates independently of government, banks are able to regulate the level of inflation. This limits governments' ability to use inflation to combine high public spending and low taxes. This can be seen as inhibiting the use of Keynesian demand management to reduce unemployment, but it can also be regarded as limiting governments' ability to bribe electorates before elections and to finance public spending by eventually unmanageable debt. This has been particularly important in debates over the role of the ECB.

There is here an important distinction between the role of government and politics in setting the overall rules of the game, on the one hand, and intervention to serve a governing party's own interests, on the other. The former is the proper realm of democracy. For example, should a central bank's mission be solely to achieve a low target level of inflation, or should it be to combine that task with trying to safeguard employment levels? This is the issue at the heart of the ECB debate. There is legitimate disagreement among economists about the virtue of both approaches, and there are successful examples of both. There would be no abuse in a government seeking parliamentary approval for a change of rule for a central bank that would then administer its revised mandate independently of political intervention. This is quite different from a central bank regime that permits governments to instruct or bully central banks to change policy from day to day, to suit their electoral needs. Rules to protect the integrity of such institutions might well include protection of the market, where governments are manipulating economic variables to secure support, but the principal aim is to design institutions that secure democracy's own future.

Similar principles apply to the autonomy of national statistical and information services. Their integrity is essential if citizens are to know what is happening in their societies, especially as social media are increasingly being used to distort facts and present false realities. They often lack the status of the judiciary and central banks, and their existence is often not widely understood. They therefore have more difficulty defending themselves from political abuse, but any instances of tampering with their integrity serve as litmus tests of a political system on its way to corruption. Related to this is the need for the professional autonomy of scientists and journalists, including broadcasting media and new social media. These face attacks from several sources: from governments, from wealthy proprietors and sponsors, and most recently from the alt. right's denigration of the idea of knowledge. Democracy needs rules about transparency and the honesty of information, as only these can guarantee the informed debate and organization of opposition on which future, seriously contested elections depend.

Unlike residents of other parts of the world, citizens of EU member states have a further line of protection from abuse by their governments in rights of appeal to various EU institutions, especially the ECJ. Because the EU consists of states with a wide range of political governments, a range that is changing all the time as elections bring political change to individual countries, it can never be captured by any one political family, and is therefore less vulnerable to abuse than any individual nation. This is a precious addition to the armoury of democracy protection. It is, for example, the EU that is trying with some success to prevent interference with the rule of law in Hungary and Poland.

In post-democracy, institutions that protect citizens from governments, like the voting system itself, remain in place. However, if citizens are not vigilant – and a lack of vigilance is a key symptom of post-democracy – they can become falsely reassuring shells, behind which anti-democratic manipulation can flourish. It is not reasonable to expect the mass of ordinary citizens to exercise that kind of vigilance. We therefore depend massively on organizations and informal groups, often surviving on shoe-string budgets, that make it their business to keep a sharp watch on what governments are doing, and to blow loud whistles when they suspect abuse.

One of my key messages in *Post-Democracy* was that, in the last analysis, the health of democracy depends on active citizens, on ourselves; parties, government and the other political institutions alone cannot guarantee it. I was speaking mainly of the need for groups in civil society from time to time to rock the complacency of public life. However, the same point applies to those institutions to which we look to ensure that democratic institutions themselves are not abused. They too need active, sometimes irritating, even busy-body, groups and movements that look to their health.

Reviving Democratic Alternatives

Despite, or indeed because of, these challenges, we have to work hard to revive democracy. As Sophie van Bijsterveld (2002) has argued, we are living in an age of transition, when much about the institutions that we thought we could take for granted, such as the sovereign nation-state, are becoming fluid and subject to change. Much of this change is in the control of rich and powerful groups and individuals, primarily transnational corporations. There is a strong temptation for ordinary citizens and the institutions we have created, including political parties, to respond by defensively holding on to what we have.

Beyond Post-Democracy?

But there lies the false security of pessimistic nostalgia. We have to develop flexible and imaginative solutions of our own. In *Post-Democracy*, I argued that this kind of innovation would depend on social movements emerging from civil society, articulating issues being neglected by post-democratic politics, trying to force their attentions on parties caught up in it. This remains true, despite the confusion of 'Astroturf' movements created by IT, and I come back to that approach now.

The vital role of civil society movements as the places where citizens with moral integrity could 'live in truth' was a major theme of Václav Havel during his long, persecuted years in state-socialist Czechoslovakia following the collapse of the Prague Spring in 1968. Oddly, in his 1978 essay 'The power of the powerless' he called such movements 'post-democratic' (Havel 1987a). By this term, he meant the opposite of my own usage, referring to informal groups of concerned and powerless citizens, who, by determinedly living in and insisting on truthfulness could eventually have some impact on power. Although we are using terms in opposite ways, and although he was living in a completely different and far bleaker society, our understanding of civil society and its role are the same. Indeed, in his essay 'Conscience and politics', Havel (1987b) showed extraordinary prescience in seeing that western societies were not so different from those of the Soviet bloc in being dominated by consumerism and the impersonal rationalization of formal structures, to the exclusion of a politics based on ethical concerns and human values.

There is a barrier to fruitful cooperation between parties and civil society movements in their mutual dislike. The former see the latter as disruptive, likely to raise issues that will be unpopular with voters, and 'wasting' political resources that could be more fruitfully used in election campaigns. Movements, in their turn, see party people as traitors who systematically let down or, at best, compromise the causes they adopt. In reality, they need each other. Parties trying to bring together disparate constituencies to form large electoral blocks have to be careful about the risks they take with new and unfamiliar policies. But if they are too cautious and fail to spot trends emerging in the population, they will be left behind – which is currently happening to Europe's former major parties. Social movements can and do take the risks; and parties can learn from their experience, adopting themes that clearly have a purchase in the wider electorate, and ignoring those that do not. The relationship is similar to that between large corporations and small entrepreneurial firms in high-tech sectors. The latter try new ventures; some fail and drop by the wayside; those that succeed are likely to be taken up by the larger corporations. This is not an analogy that many social movements will find attractive, but it probably represents their main chance of developing ideas that both find real practical success in public policy and contribute to the rejuvenation of mainstream politics.

Old party structures and loyalties are fragmenting. It is highly unlikely that existing organizations and their personnel will be able radically to improve their situation purely from within. They have to be open to new influences, often from groups with whom they feel uncomfortable, outsiders trying to burst into the polite conversations of existing insiders. In recent decades, we have seen major examples of exactly how that process can work. Unfortunately, those examples teach some disturbing lessons. In *Post-Democracy* I listed environmental and feminist groups alongside xenophobic ones as movements capable of disturbing the complacency of post-democracy. Existing parties have tried to respond to the latter two (feminism and xenophobia), not so much to environmentalism. During the 1990s, most west European social democratic parties (and the US Democrats) perceived that their traditional industrial working-class constituencies were declining, and in seeking to refresh their relations with a changing society they listened to movements expressing resentment at exclusion on behalf of women, as well as ethnic and sexual minorities. They developed policies on behalf of these groups, and were often successful in attracting their votes. However, at least partly because this same shift in emphasis ran alongside social democracy's flirtation with neoliberalism, it also brought a neglect of both the concerns of the old constituencies and material inequality. Inequality was redefined in a neoliberal manner to mean the elimination of barriers to advance for some individuals in disadvantaged categories. The newly neglected, mainly manual, working men then began to join the ranks of the pessimistically nostalgic.

More recently, established parties on the moderate right have been listening to movements expressing that nostalgia. The US Republicans have done this, though with ambiguous success, by endorsing Donald Trump. The Austrian ÖVP, discussed in Chapter 5, is another case. A once stolid and declining orthodox Christian democratic and conservative party rapidly transformed itself into a xenophobic nationalistic one, and immediately reaped electoral rewards. We can expect more west European conservative movements to imitate their example. In central Europe, the similar example of Fidesz in Hungary is already being widely followed. Sections of some parties on the left across Europe are also seeing what they can learn from the revival of nationalism.

It cannot therefore be claimed that the established parties have remained complacently aloof in their post-democratic cocoons, though we are of course at liberty to criticize the particular solutions they find. More important at the present time is to note that there is no end to history in this process, but continuing dialectic. Social democratic and other centre-left parties did find a solution to the problem of a declining working-class electorate, but thereby stoked the fires of a resurgence of the xenophobic right. What reactions will now be generated against the rise of the alt.right? What groups, interests and values are being excluded by the new nationalism, what movements are emerging in civil society to express them, and through what means are these likely to be articulated and shaped into alternatives? For the purposes of the present volume, we are concerned not so much with the substance of any new political agendas, but with their contribution to renovating democracy. Democracy cannot thrive if society provides us with only one powerful set of political emotions and preferences. Despite the words of Private Willis's ditty, 'Nature' cannot be relied upon to do this for us. Work has to be done through civil society and social movements. Democracy in the twenty-first century will no longer be able to rely on strong party identities forged in past struggles, but it can find new kinds of bases.

Neither neoliberalism nor the alt.right consists of an overwhelmingly attractive sets of ideas. Purely neoliberal parties as such have usually been small; neoliberals have depended for their wider support on appropriating first conservative and Christian, later social democratic, parties and the stronger identities that these have lent to the neoliberal project. The alt.right has a more solid appeal to social identity than neoliberals, and it is not yet clear whether this is a movement that is still growing or whether it is reaching a peak. It was widely expected to make a major breakthrough in the 2019 European parliamentary elections. Steve Bannon, a close associate of Donald Trump and of some US billionaire alt.right backers, tried (ironically, from the US) to organize an international grouping of European nationalist parties, and it was widely assumed that the Russian government would also be assisting some anti-EU nationalists. In the event, Bannon's attempted grouping fell apart. It is not easy to calculate the eventual exact strength of alt. right parties in the elections. The main alt.right groups of parties did better than in the previous election (in 2014), but some parties that one would define as far right had been independent of groups at that time. Overall, the alt.right as a whole seemed to achieve around 25 per cent of the popular vote, against a little over 20 per cent in 2014. This was higher than the score of any of the *individual* non-alt.right groups, but smaller than conservative and liberal groups (34 per cent) and social democratic, socialist and green groups (36.7 per cent) taken together. As of today, the xenophobic right does not have the degree of popular support that would justify the panic it is causing in other political groups. The vulnerabilities of neoliberals and the xenophobic right are such that their opponents should be emboldened to confront them. Practical, positive values have to be articulated. No nation can turn back in on itself and hide from the world; but neither should anyone be exposed to the disruptive forces of globalization without protection. But this protection cannot be provided by individual states alone. International cooperation is needed – to extract taxation from globally mobile giant high-tech firms and other large corporations, to tackle destruction of a climate that does not acknowledge national boundaries, to prevent speculative international finance from destabilizing the world. These are not difficult ideas to explain, and they embody values that almost everyone can see are urgent and important to our lives. Similarly, the great majority of people can understand the dangers presented by political leaders who seek to override institutions that protect the rights of ordinary citizens.

Fear and hate are the most human powerful emotions, more essential to the survival of species in primitive conditions than love and cooperation – except to the extent that the survival of the young depends on nurture. This was of course a role consigned mainly to women. However, survival in the complex human tasks of modern society requires cooperation; innovation and enterprise depend on willingness to explore combinations across cultures and openness to working with 'outsiders'; a satisfying life requires caring and love. Pessimistic nostalgia's incitement of rejection and exclusion of apparent invaders of our space may be powerful, but many people, probably even a large majority, may react negatively to them, or at least to the turbulence and violence they threaten. It is not difficult for people to understand that we cannot live without accepting our mutual dependence. Therefore, although at present little seems to withstand the rising tide of pessimistically nostalgic feelings, optimistic, inclusive, outward-looking emotions, as well as rationality itself, have their own power. If democracy is to recover strength, these alternatives need to find means for their own powerfully motivating expression. This requires both stressing the virtues of positive values and pointing unflinchingly to the road on which the politics of pessimistic nostalgia is taking us. The populations of the first half of the twentieth century who were attracted by ideologies of hatred advocated by the left and right alike possibly had the excuse that they did not know where such approaches might lead – though European history was replete with revolutionary violence, pogroms and holocausts that might have warned them. We now know what happened to those ideologies. The numbers of our contemporaries likely to follow movements of that political family for long will be augmented only if they do not realize the direction in which they are being urged to travel, and if some among those who do not share such ideas feel they need to compromise with them – and therefore further legitimate them – because of their growing popularity.

The twin barriers to realization of these optimistic possibilities are the impact of waves of refugees from North Africa and the Middle East, among whom there is a tiny number of terrorists, and the use that only the extremely rich can make of this phenomenon through manipulation of social media to advance causes of the extreme right. Every one of the cases of a rapid growth of pessimistic nostalgic movements in western countries has been powered by waves of refugees and immigrants – or by fears that such waves might arrive. The capacity of the manipulators of mass media, both traditional and

IT-based, to stir up a frenzy of fear and hatred may not yet have run its course. It may well be that in the end we shall depend on some members of the liberal super-rich to fund rival campaigns exploiting the terrifying possibilities of these instruments. This may be necessary, but it will remain unsatisfactory, as it continues to assume citizens who are essentially a *tabula rasa*, vulnerable to responding passively to whatever influences are most successively imposed on them.

There must also be an alternative, the development of a population capable of evaluating and checking what purports to be knowledge and evidence, of using the Internet discriminatingly, and reflecting on the tangle of contradictory values in which we are all involved but must find our own ways through. People will still reach a wide diversity of conclusions as a result of these processes, but that is democracy. All we can ask, but we must find ways of insisting on it, is that citizens have had a chance to use their own abilities to think and ponder.

This is essentially a matter of education, as this is the process through which we learn to think and ponder. It is a notable fact that, in almost all countries where the relevant research has been conducted, the more education a person has received, the less they are likely to support alt.right movements. Of course, some highly educated people do support them, because their deeply held, rationally considered and coherently argued values are socially conservative. Their ability to do so is part of the diversity that liberal democracy must always support. But one is entitled to assume that vast sums are being spent on the manipulation of communications because those spending the money believe that they will not have adequate support in the population at large unless they do so, and therefore that developing the capacity of citizens to use their critical faculties in the face of such communications would reduce support for the causes they advocate.

To some extent this is a process that can be left to itself. The proportion of populations experiencing advanced secondary and tertiary education is constantly expanding, and this more or less automatically increases the proportion of the population capable of evaluating evidence and reflecting on their own ideas. However, the needs of early twenty-first-century democracy require setting the bar a little higher than simply increasing the numbers of the generally educated. Working out a sensible position on issues like climate change and what can be done about refugees requires an ability and a willingness to take politically relevant knowledge seriously. Meanwhile, not only are those with the power to do so eager to obfuscate our search for such knowledge through the tricks of post-truth, but the political parties that used to process knowledge for us are losing our trust.

All this places a heavy burden on everyone involved in communication, from teachers at all levels, to journalists, social media bloggers, ministers of religion, trade union officials and many others. What are we doing, not so much to impart specific values, but to help our fellow citizens to think critically, to check and to evaluate? For several of these groups, this responsibility is becoming more difficult to fulfil, largely as a result of the victories of neoliberalism. For example, education, including higher education, is in many countries being instrumentalized. Young people are being encouraged to regard their education as a mechanical process of working to achieve high scores in examinations in order to be able to earn high salaries. Systems like the British and American ones, that require most university students to acquire heavy debts during their years of study in order to pay fees and maintenance costs, are encouraging this process more than others. It creates the danger of an educated population that is trained not to think and reach conclusions based on evidence, but merely to perform in tests. Journalists, whether working in print or audiovisual media, are under pressure to achieve high levels of readership or viewership in order to boost corporate profits, and this leads them to seek the lowest common denominator of pumping out unchallenging material that makes few demands on thought. In countries where the alt.right has not yet achieved dominance, it may be possible for the improvement of citizens' general competence to be an objective of public policy. But even there, the central message remains: we all have a responsibility as citizens to work for these things in our daily lives.

Changing Formal Politics

True though this is, individuals can do little without larger movements. In particular, what kinds of movement are likely to refresh our party systems and public life in general? All three of the movements I listed in *Post-Democracy* as disturbing the complacency of post-democracy – environmentalist, feminist and xenophobic – have acquired greater salience and broader importance than I had envisaged in 2003. Considerable space has been devoted in these pages to the last of these, but the other two now demand attention.

The revival of environmentalism

The first wave of green movements – in the 1980s and 1990s, the most dynamic new forces emerging from citizens' movements into party politics – had for some years been in decline, partly because of disappointing performances by green parties in government, partly because the financial crisis seemed to nullify the urgency of environmental issues. The tide now seems to be turning: green movements and parties are recovering strength in a number of countries. Increasing numbers of voters are seeing them not just as defenders of the environment, but also as the most reliable opponents of the alt.right. Some of the reasons for this may in themselves be negative – the intensifying menace of climate change, the domination of politics in the US, Brazil and elsewhere by business interests denying the reality of a human role in that menace, and the ambivalence of some liberal and social democratic parties on immigration and related issues – but the new political energy being generated, particularly among young people, contributes to democratic renewal as well as helping to save our planet. The development of an international movement among schoolchildren demanding action to save the planet has been the most positive development in public life for many years.

Environmental activism can be of the political right (with an emphasis on preserving natural and human heritage) or left (stressing the role of capitalist profit in destroying the environment). Both could slip into pessimistic nostalgia, seeking to preserve the way of life of existing wealthy societies against the spread of economic activities across the world. But nearly all current green movements are avoiding this and stress the scope for environmental entrepreneurialism and for public and private action to use technological advance to produce cleaner, more energy-efficient economies. Green movements appeal primarily to people holding certain values rather than to interests, and this will remain a weakness, preventing them from becoming dominant political forces. However, as we have seen, interests alone are not the exclusive supports of political identity that too many political scientists believe. Identity is rooted in a complex amalgam of interests and values, and the alt.right is currently making better use of this than most other political forces. If today we are seeing a revival of value-based, 'first-axis' issues, then value-oriented political causes, prominently among them environmentalism, have a future.

Green movements provide a major base for powerful critiques of both alt.right and neoliberal values, the former for its attacks on science and deliberate lack of concern for the future as well as its rejection of international collaboration, the latter for its denial of the need for collective action and rejection of human cooperation outside the frame of the market. Existing parties wishing to benefit from the energy being generated by environmentalism must therefore resist temptations to associate themselves with either pessimistic nostalgia or neoliberalism. It can be objected that it is only younger, better educated citizens who tend to care about these issues. But these are vital groups in any electorate, well worth winning away from rivals.

The potentiality of gender politics

It was suggested in Chapter 6 that gender has not been the basis of party political conflict, because men and women tend to live together. However, current conflicts over gender do not so much pit men against women as bring confrontations over different expectations of gender roles, and wider sets of values that have a relationship to gender. Many women share essentially 'masculist' values, while many men hold feminist ones. Masculism is an important component of pessimistic nostalgia; feminism of its nemesis. A masculist agenda includes nostalgia for industrial society. Seen most clearly in the political approach of Donald Trump, this combines despair at the loss of the white male society associated with industrial work, hostility to globalization (and, by extension, immigrants and ethnic minorities), which are seen as instrumental in industrial decline, and resentment at the encroachment of women into occupational and public life, mainly in the services sectors that have replaced industrial work. The further extremes of masculism take us to that association with violence that is an important potential ingredient of pessimistic nostalgia. A willingness to engage in fighting is often seen as a highly masculine characteristic, including violence against women. It is no coincidence that in recent years misogyny and even femicide have become politicized terms.

The ultimate expression of violent masculism as hostility to feminism is the use of rape and threats to rape, often directed against prominent feminists by the wilder fringes of the alt.right. Carl Benjamin, a candidate in the 2019 European parliamentary elections for the British anti-EU and anti-Islamic party UKIP, achieved publicity for asserting that he 'would not even rape' Jess Phillips, a feminist and pro-EU Labour MP. Benjamin has also claimed that feminism is to blame for many men feeling worthless. A less marginal and more serious example is Vox, the Spanish alt.right party that went from having 0.2 per cent of the national vote in 2016 to 10.3 per cent in 2019. It campaigns on three main issues: hostility against Islam, against moves for Catalan independence and against feminism. Prominent in this last has been its support for a group of young men, known as *la manada* (the wolf pack), found guilty of the gang rape of a girl in Pamplona. The case has been highly controversial, Spaniards being divided over whether they support the victim of the rape or the men who perpetrated it, the dispute being, as often in rape cases, over the level of presumed consent. Vox has politicized the controversy. One might also include in the issue of attitudes to rape the move by opponents of abortion in the US also to oppose abortions for women whose pregnancy is the result of rape. In the state of Alabama, which recently legislated to that effect, a rapist also has rights to claim custody over children resulting from the assault. This seems to imply a desire to protect the right of rapists to control women's bodies even after the event itself.

The importance of gender politics is strengthened by the fact that gender, at first sight a 'first-axis' issue, is closely related to second-axis, class ones. A major error in my argument in *Post-Democracy* was to assert that the classes of post-industrial societies were not developing a consciousness of themselves, while I also stated that gender was an example of an issue that defied the logic of post-democracy. Compared with industrial society, most of the sectors of post-industrialism have large female workforces, and in general women occupy the more junior, men the more senior roles in these. It is also characteristic of post-industrial economies that while both members of many heterosexual couples have jobs in the paid workforce, the strain of combining both professional and domestic responsibilities tends to be borne more heavily by women. In important respects therefore, consciousness of class identity and the development of class-based political agendas increasingly take the form of gender consciousness and gendered issues.

The original labour movement was essentially a male phenomenon, which interpreted the problems of all working people through the eyes of 'breadwinner' men. In post-industrial society, many of their problems may be best articulated by women or at least through a feminine perspective. Women experience more keenly not only issues of work–life balance, but also precariousness in the labour market, deficiencies in care services through declining public spending, and the manipulation of consumers by corporations. These are problems that men share, but it needs the confident politicized female identity that is currently taking shape in many societies to propel them on to the political agenda and thereby revitalize democracy. The great error of social democracy's adoption of feminist (as well as ethnic minority, gay rights and disability) causes in the 1990s was to see these as means of escaping from historical commitments to a broader, material egalitarianism and of avoiding confronting issues of corporate power, whether in relations with employees or with customers. The exact opposite is needed if social democracy is to recover its position as a major political force.

Today, the majority of trade union members in almost all western countries are women, and unions remain the most important potentially political organizations that have been created by working people. But, almost everywhere, unions are losing members, which is one major cause of the decline of an active presence of ordinary working people in contemporary politics, and hence a cause of post-democracy. A revival of unions, or similar movements if that particular form of employee organization is seen as outmoded, is necessary if that presence is to be revived. This requires overcoming serious conflicts of interest that divide, for example, workers in secure jobs and often with union representation from those in precarious jobs or false self-employment; or workers in traditionally unionized sectors like manufacturing and public services from those in most private services sectors who have never seen unions as relevant to their employment problems. A female-led unionism is not the sole answer to these divisions, but it makes an important contribution, as it can addresses issues that are of importance to workers across the full range of modern sectors and types of employment.

Women are found in large numbers working in the public and care services that embody values that are the main challenges to both neoliberal and alt.right worldviews. These are values and themes that belong to the left, centre and non-neoliberal right as much as nation does to the far right. They also belong primarily to the first axis of political conflict, while also relating deeply to the more material second one. There are fascinating links here with the findings of Daniel Oesch discussed in the previous chapter. He found that people engaged on interpersonal tasks were the most likely to be liberal-minded. He stresses that gender was not a factor in explaining these differences, but in most societies women are more likely to be employed in interpersonal work roles than in administrative or technical ones.

West European women are less likely than men to vote for pessimistic nostalgic causes and parties – though the same is not true of white women in the US. This has led to a major reversal of the twentieth-century pattern, whereby women tended to vote to the right of men. Terri Givens (2004), the main researcher in this field, finds this to be mainly related to the greater numbers of men found in manual-working occupations, often the main predictor of extreme-right voting. Her research was limited to Austria, France and German, and predates the most recent rise of alt.right parties, but her findings have considerable resonance in recent developments in the alt. right. These kinds of male workers are in irreversible historical decline, which is why they are attracted by pessimistic nostalgia for its full bundle of causes: rejection of globalization, hostility to immigrants and resentment at women's changing roles. It should however be possible for some of them to see the value of new agendas of work-related issues that are not limited to their own declining industries, and also to appreciate that the alt.right does not address these. All it offers is the aggravation of resentment, about which its leaders plan to do nothing substantial.

Previous chapters have shown how, across the advanced world, the state of democracy is darker than it was at the start of the century, when I wrote *Post-Democracy*. We have certainly moved several paces further down the road towards post-democracy during that time. Our politics could be taken over by a few billionaires and governments manipulating social media to stir up various forms of hatred and distract attention from the activities of unregulated capitalism. At the same time, the prospects for renewing and changing the popular roots of political conflict also seem more open and encouraging – there seem now to be more possibilities of taking steps back up the road away from post-democracy. The new divisions over values, dangerous though they are, have democratic potential. There is evidence that many people, particularly younger and more educated ones, oppose what is happening. Women are increasingly defining political agendas in the widest sense. The young and educated can easily slide into a self-satisfied individualism, as neoliberalism encourages them to do. But many resist that temptation and care about what is going on around them, and the ranks of the educated are steadily increasing. They provide the background against which more active groups organize, publicize, campaign. Provided they exist, continue to reproduce themselves, and receive from millions of others what they need to flourish – money, demonstrators in the street, active volunteers – democracy will revive.

References

Amato, M. and Fantacci, L. 2012 [2009]. *The End of Finance*. Cambridge: Polity.
Amato, M. and Fantacci, L. 2014 [2012]. *Saving the Market from Capitalism: Ideas for an Alternative Finance*. Cambridge: Polity.
Bastagli, F., Coady, D. and Gupta, S. 2012. 'Income inequality and fiscal policy', IMF Staff Discussion Note SDN/12/08. Washington, DC: IMF.
Bonefeld, W. 2017. *The Strong State and the Free Economy*. Lanham, MD: Rowman & Littlefield.
Bork, R. H. 1993 [1978]. *The Antitrust Paradox: A Policy at War with Itself*, 2nd edn. New York: Free Press.
Brown, G. 2018. 'Gordon Brown in dire warning about the next financial crisis', https://www.bbc.co.uk/news/business-45504521.
Callaghan, H. 2018. *Contestants, Profiteers and the Political Dynamics of Marketization*. Oxford: Oxford University Press.
Campanella, E. and Dassù, M. 2019. *Anglo Nostalgia: The Politics of Emotion in a Fractured West*. London: Hurst and Co.
Chakrabortty, A. 2012. 'Why do bankers get to decide who pays for the mess Europe is in?', *Guardian*, 2 April.
Chakrabortty, A. 2018. 'Ten years after Lehmans, it's as if we've learned nothing from the crash', *Guardian*, 5 September.

Crouch, C. 2002. *Coping with Post-Democracy*. London: Fabian Society.
Crouch, C. 2003. *Post-Democracy*. Cambridge: Polity.
Crouch, C. 2015a. *The Knowledge Corrupters*. Cambridge: Polity.
Crouch, C. 2015b. 'Can there be a normative theory of corporate political power?', in V. Schneider and B. Eberlein (eds), *Complex Democracy: Varieties, Crises, and Transformations*. Berlin: Springer, 117–31.
Crouch, C. 2016a. 'Capitalism, inequality and democracy', *Stato e Mercato*, 2: 159–82.
Crouch, C. 2016b. *Society and Social Change in 21st Century Europe*. London: Palgrave Macmillan.
Crouch, C. 2018. *The Globalization Backlash*. Cambridge: Polity.
Dahl, R. A. 1961. *Who Governs? Democracy and Power in an American City*. New Haven, CT: Yale University Press.
Dahl, R. A. 1971. *Polyarchy, Participation and Opposition*. New Haven, CT: Yale University Press.
Dahl, R. A. 1982. *Dilemmas of Pluralist Democracy: Autonomy Versus Control*. New Haven, CT: Yale University Press.
Diamond, S. 1995. *Roads to Dominion: Right-Wing Movements and Political Power in the United States*. New York: Guilford Press.
Driver, C. and Thompson, G. (eds) 2018. *Corporate Governance in Contention*. Oxford: Oxford University Press.
Economist Intelligence Unit, annual. *Democracy Index*. London: The Economist.
Edwards, F. R. 1999. 'Hedge funds and the collapse of long-term capital management', *Journal of Economic Perspectives*, 13/2: 189–210.
Edwards, F. R. and Mishkin, F. S. 1995. *The Decline of Traditional Banking: Implications for Financial Stability and Regulatory Policy*, NBER Working Paper 4993. Cambridge, MA: National Bureau for Economic Research.
Elsässer, L., Hense, S. and Schäfer, A. 2018. *Government of the People, by the Elite, for the Rich*. MPIfG Discussion Paper 18/5. Cologne: Max Planck Institute for the Study of Societies.
Fama, E. 1970. 'Efficient capital markets: a review of theory and empirical work', *Journal of Finance*, 25/2: 383–417.

References

Feher, M. 2018. *Rated Agency: Investee Politics in a Speculative Age*. New York: Zone Books.

Fligstein, N. and Shin, T. 2007. 'Shareholder value and the transformation of the US economy, 1984–2000', *Sociological Forum*, 22/4: 399–424.

Förster, M., Llena-Nozal, A. and Nafilyan, V. 2014. *Trends in Top Incomes and Their Taxation in OECD Countries*, OECD Society, Employment and Migration Working Paper 159. Paris: OECD.

France, P. and Vauchez, A. 2017. *Sphère publique: Intérêts privés*. Paris: Sciences Po.

Froud, J., Johal, S., Papazian, V. and Williams, K. 2004. 'The temptation of Houston: a case study of financialization', *Critical Perspectives on Accounting*, 15/6–7: 885–909.

Fukuyama, F. 1992. *The End of History and the Last Man*. New York: Free Press.

Givens, T. E. 2004. 'The radical right gender gap', *Comparative Political Studies*, 37/1: 30–54.

Government of Greece, 2012. *Memorandum of Understanding on Specific Economic Policy Conditionality, 9 February 2012*. Athens: Government of Greece.

Hansard Society 2019. *Audit of Political Engagement 16*. London: Hansard Society.

Havel, V. 1987a. 'The power of the powerless', in J. Vladislav (ed.), *Vaclav Hável: Living in Truth*. London: Faber and Faber, 36–122.

Havel, V. 1987b. 'Politics and conscience', in J. Vladislav (ed.), *Vaclav Hável: Living in Truth*. London: Faber and Faber, 136–57.

Howard, P. N. and Woolley, S. C. 2018. *Computational Propaganda: Political Parties, Politicians, and Political Manipulation*. Oxford: Oxford University Press.

IMF 2010. *A Fistful of Dollars: Lobbying and the Financial Crisis*. Washington, DC: International Monetary Fund.

Johnson, S. 2009. 'The quiet coup', *Atlantic Home*, May.

Kastner, L. 2017. 'Business lobbying under salience: financial industry mobilization against the European financial transaction tax', *Journal of European Public Policy*, 25/11: 1648–66.

Kitschelt, H. and Rehm, P. 2014. 'Occupations as a site of political preference formation', *Comparative Political Studies*, 47/12: 1670–706.

Krippner, G. 2012. *Capitalizing on Crisis: The Political Origins of the Rise of Finance*. Cambridge, MA: Harvard University Press.

Kuttner, R. 2018. *Can Democracy Survive Global Capitalism?* New York: Norton.

Lindblom, C. E. 1977. *Politics and Markets*. New York: Basic Books.

MacLean, N. 2018. *Democracy in Chains*. Melbourne: Scribe.

Mair, P. 2013. *The Hollowing of Western Democracy*. London: Verso.

Mancini, P. 2011. *Between Commodification and Lifestyle Politics. Does Silvio Berlusconi Provide a New Model of Politics for the Twenty-First Century?* Oxford: Reuters Institute for the Study of Journalism.

Mény, Y. and Surel, Y. (eds.) 2001. *Democracies and the Populist Challenge*. Basingstoke: Palgrave.

Merkel, W. 2014. 'Is capitalism compatible with democracy?' *Zeitschrift für Vergleichende Politikwissenschaft*, 8: 109–28.

Mounk, J. 2018. *The People vs. Democracy: Why our Freedom Is in Danger and How to Save It*. Cambridge, MA: Harvard University Press.

Müller, J.-W. 2018. *What Is Populism?* Philadelphia: Pennsylvania University Press.

OECD 2011. *Divided We Stand: Why Inequality Keeps Rising*. Paris: OECD.

OECD 2017. 'Import content of exports', https://data.oecd.org/trade/import-content-of-exports.htm.

Oesch, D. 2006a. 'Coming to grips with a changing class structure: an analysis of employment stratification in Britain, Germany, Sweden and Switzerland', *International Sociology*, 21/2: 263–88.

Oesch, D. 2006b. *Redrawing the Class Map*. Basingstoke: Palgrave Macmillan.

Oesch, D. and Rodríguez Menés, J. 2011. 'Upgrading or polarization? Occupational change in Britain, Germany, Spain and Switzerland, 1990–2008', *Socio-Economic Review*, 9/3: 503–31.

Olson, M. 1965. *The Logic of Collective Action*. Cambridge, MA: Harvard University Press.

Pabst, A. 2016. 'Is liberal democracy sliding into democratic despotism?', *Political Quarterly*, 87/1: 91–5.

Pennacchi, L. 2018. *De valoribus disputandum est: Sui valori dopo il neoliberismo.* Milan: Mimesis.
Piketty, T. 2013. *Capital in the Twenty-First Century*, trans. A Goldhammer. Cambridge, MA: Harvard University Press.
Ponattu, D. Sachs, A. and Weineit, H. 2018. *Market Concentration and the Labour Share in Germany*, Policy brief 2018/03. Gütersloh: Bertelsmann Stiftung.
Posner, R. A. 2001. *Antitrust Law*, 2nd edn. Chicago, IL: University of Chicago Press.
Potter, R. A. 2018. *Report of Brookings Series on Regulatory Process and Perspectives*. Washington, DC: Brookings Institution.
Reiff, M. R. 2013. *Exploitation and Economic Justice in the Liberal Capitalist State*. Oxford: Oxford University Press.
Runciman, D. 2018. *How Democracy Ends*. London: Profile Books.
Shiller, R. J. 2000. *Irrational Exuberance*. Princeton, NJ: Princeton University Press.
Social Enterprise UK 2012. *The Shadow State*. London: Social Enterprise UK.
Steele, S., Ruskin, G., Sarcevic, L. and Stuckler, D. 2019. 'Are industry-funded charities promoting "advocacy-led studies" or "evidence-based science"? A case study of the International Life Sciences Institute', *Globalization and Health* 15.
Steenvoorden, E. and Harteveld, E. 2017. 'The appeal of nostalgia: the influence of societal pessimism on support for populist radical right parties', *West European Politics*, 41/1: 28–52.
Streeck, W. 2017 [2013]. *Buying Time: The Delayed Crisis of Democratic Capitalism*, 2nd edn., trans. P. Camiller. London: Verso.
Streeck, W. 2015a. 'Comment on Wolfgang Merkel, "Is capitalism compatible with democracy?"', *Zeitschrift für Vergleichende Politikwissenschaft*, 9/1.
Streeck, W. 2015b. 'Heller, Schmitt and the Euro', *European Law Journal*, 21/3: 361–70.
Susskind, J. 2018. *Future Politics*. Oxford: Oxford University Press.
Tooze, A. 2018. *Crashed: How a Decade of Financial Crises Changed the World*. London: Allen Lane.

UK Electoral Commission 2018. *Spending on Digital Campaign Activity*. London: Electoral Commission.
US Supreme Court 2010. *Citizens United v. Federal Election Commission*, 08-205. Washington, DC: US Supreme Court.
US Supreme Court 2014. *McCutcheon v. Federal Election Commission*, 12-536. Washington, DC: US Supreme Court.
van Bijsterveld, S. 2002. *The Empty Throne: Democracy and the Rule of Law in Transition*. Utrecht: Lemma Publishers.
van der Zwan, N. 2014. 'Making sense of financialization', *Socio-Economic Review*, 12/1: 99–129.
Watt, A. and Watzka, S. 2018. *Overcoming Euro Area Fragility*, IMK Report 139. Frankfurt and Main: Hans Böckler Stiftung.
Welch, S. 2013. *Hyperdemocracy*. Basingstoke, Palgrave Macmillan.
Ziblatt, D. and Levitsky, S. 2018. *How Democracies Die*. New York: Broadway Books.

Index

abortion, 102, 124, 162
academic freedom, 106–7
accounting practices, 42, 49–50
advertising, 10, 27, 126, 145–6
Afghanistan, 35
Al Qaida, 98
alt.right, 97–116, 137, 140, 142–5, 147–8, 153–60, 162, 164–5
Amazon, 31, 35
anti-Semitism, 93, 99–100
anti-vax movement, 103, 145
Arthur Andersen, 49–50
auditing, 42, 47, 49–50
Aufstehen, 95, 96
austerity, 76, 135, 138
Austria, 96, 98, 108–9, 135, 153, 165
Austro-Hungarian Empire, 106
authoritarianism, 6, 15, 17, 134

automotive industry, 30
aviation industry, 30, 33

bank bailouts, 52–3, 55, 56
Bank of England, 55–6
bankruptcies, 49–50, 51–2
banks, 32, 41, 42–65, 66–7, 74–5, 78–9, 80, 83, 88, 148
   see also financial sector
Banks, Arron, 114
Bannon, Steve, 154
Basel Committee on Banking Supervision (BCBS), 54
Belgium, 9, 92, 96, 128
Benjamin, Carl, 162
Berlusconi, Silvio, 10–11, 24, 73, 80–1
Boeing, 33
Bolsonaro, Jair, 100
Bonefeld, Werner, 85–6
Brazil, 96, 100–1, 159
Bretton Woods system, 42–3, 69–70, 86–7

Index

Brexit, 12, 27–8, 85, 92, 98, 100, 108, 111–16, 137, 143, 146, 147
Britain *see* United Kingdom
British Broadcasting Corporation (BBC), 57
Brown, Gordon, 52, 57
building societies, 51
Bulgaria, 96, 107
Bundesbank, 70
Bush, George W., 17, 35, 49
Bush, Jeb, 17
business regulation, 7, 26–7, 33, 39, 141

Cadwalladr, Carole, 27
Calderoli, Roberto, 110
Callaghan, Helen, 43
Cambridge Analytica, 27, 114
Campanella, Edoardo, 92
capital movements, 46, 86–7
capital punishment, 102, 103
capitalism, 7, 32–3, 39–40, 50, 84–5, 130, 142, 160, 165
Carillion, 37
Catalonia, 162
Catholic Church, 6, 98, 99, 107, 121, 123, 124, 131, 133
central banks, 54, 55–6, 67, 70–1, 83, 148–9
Central European University, Budapest, 106–7
Chakrabortty, Aditya, 75
charismatic leaders, 20, 101–2
Charlottesville rally (2017), 100
Cheney, Richard, 35
Chicago School, 39

Chile, 39
China, 15, 39, 45, 57
Christian democracy *see* democracy, Christian
Christian Democratic Party (Italy), 127
Christian fundamentalism, 101, 102
Christianity, 6, 93, 101, 102, 106, 121, 123, 124–5, 130, 131
civil society, 21, 27, 28, 39, 81, 146, 150, 151–4
civil wars, 121, 130
clandestine opinion manipulation, 26–8, 114, 144–6, 156–7, 165
classical economic theory, 28–30, 43
clientelism, 73
climate change, 26, 88, 89, 101, 103, 145, 155, 159
clothing and textile sector, 71, 72
collective action, 23–4, 26, 160
collective bargaining, 23, 75
colonialism, 15, 111
communism, 9, 10, 15–17, 121, 122, 128
Communist Party (Italy), 10, 11, 128
company law, 43, 49
company valuation, 45, 48–9
competition, 28, 29–34, 39, 63, 85
competitiveness, 70, 72, 76, 77
compulsory voting, 9
conservatism, 15, 26, 87, 91–117, 121, 123–9, 131–9, 147–8, 153, 155

Index

Conservative Party (UK), 107, 113–14, 137
consultancy, 34–5, 47, 49
consumer choice, 29, 31, 37–8
consumer credit, 46–7, 50–1, 61–2, 142
consumer welfare, 29, 31
contraception, 124
contract allocation, 36–8, 142
core constituencies, 10, 126
corporate governance, 43–4
corporate neoliberalism, 31–2, 39–40
corporate social responsibility, 40
corporations
  accounting practices, 42, 49–50
  auditing of, 42, 47, 49–50
  and competition, 28, 29–34, 39
  executive remuneration, 44
  and globalization, 6, 7, 88
  governance, 43–4
  IT sector corporations, 30–1
  lobbying by, 25, 32, 34–6, 38, 43, 49, 65, 141
  and neoliberalism, 7, 28–40
  political funding by, 10, 25, 49
  and political influence, 24–5, 31–2, 34–6, 65
  regulation of, 7, 26–7, 33, 39, 141
  relationship to governments, 7, 28–9, 31–40, 65, 141, 142
  research and development activities, 44
  research funding by, 26–7, 62–3
  revolving door personnel movements, 35, 58, 60
  rise of giant transnational corporations, 6, 7, 24, 30
  taxation of, 7, 22–3, 46, 155
  'too big to fail', 32, 37, 55, 63, 79
  valuation of, 45, 48–9
corruption, 10–11, 14, 16, 19–20, 28–38, 73, 76, 116, 117, 141, 142
cosmopolitanism, 107, 133
courts, 14, 17, 49, 96, 105–6, 112, 114, 147–8
creationism, 103, 145
credit ratings agencies, 54
critical evaluation, 157–8
crony capitalism, 33
currency devaluation, 71, 72, 73, 77
currency markets, 42–3, 70–1, 77, 86
currency values, 42–3, 69–73, 77, 81–2
Czech Republic/Czechoslovakia, 96, 107, 122, 151

Dalberg-Acton, John, Lord Acton, 14
Dassù, Marta, 92
data harvesting, 26, 27, 114
death penalty, 102, 103
debate, 3–4, 13–14, 16, 20–1, 89, 95, 141, 147
defence sector, 32, 35, 58
deforestation, 101
de-globalization, 87–8
demand management, 40, 68–9, 81, 148

democracy
  Christian, 6, 121, 125, 126–9, 136, 153
  direct, 11–12, 101
  illiberal, 116
  indirect, 84
  liberal, 11–16, 19, 20–1, 87, 120–1, 135–6
  neoliberalism as threat to, 139–43
  people's, 15–17
  representative, 11–13, 116
  social, 5, 28, 32, 58, 76, 87, 96, 121, 123, 126–33, 136, 139, 148, 152–5, 160, 163
democratic institutions, 3, 16–17, 89, 117, 136, 150
democratic moments, 4–6, 18
Democratic Party (US), 130–2, 152
Democratici, I, 128
Denmark, 92, 96, 108
deregulation, 41–65, 74, 83, 104–5, 140–1
Deutsche Gewerkschaftsbund, 80
Deutsche Mark, 70
dictatorships, 16, 17, 19, 39, 73, 100, 121, 122, 135–6
digital stock markets, 44, 57
distorted markets, 61, 62
distribution networks, 30
diversity, 13, 104, 157
divorce, 124
Dodd-Frank Act, 54
dollar, 42, 69–70
dot-com crisis, 48–9, 50

East Asian debt crisis, 48
economic inequality, 19, 20–8, 32, 38, 65, 88, 89, 131–3, 135–7, 142, 153
economic sovereignty, 86
education, 5, 52, 74, 134, 157–8, 165–6
Edwards, Franklin, 48
egalitarianism, 104, 132, 163
Eisenhower, Dwight, 21
election campaigns, 1–2, 10, 25, 49, 108
electoral turnout, 8–9, 17–18, 84, 106, 125, 126
energy sector, 30, 32, 35, 49, 76
engineering sector, 72
Enron, 49–50
environment, 26, 64, 88, 89, 101, 132
environmentalism, 11, 117, 132, 152, 159–61
Estonia, 96
ethnic minorities, 97, 98, 100, 101, 103–4, 115, 137, 153, 161
euro, 53, 66–8, 70–8, 81–2, 83, 140
European Central Bank (ECB), 55–6, 68, 71, 74, 75–82, 83, 148
European Commission (EC), 73, 75–82, 84
European Council, 84
European Court of Justice (ECJ), 33, 63, 113, 149
European customs union, 113
European Parliament, 79, 80, 83–4, 85–6, 89
European single market, 113
European Union (EU), 7, 17, 34, 46, 54, 60, 66–90, 104, 107, 110, 134, 149

see also Brexit
Eurozone crisis, 53, 66–90, 135, 140
Exchange Rate Mechanism (ERM), 70
executive remuneration, 44
expertise, 37, 38, 50, 61–3, 64, 144–5
see also knowledge

fake news, 144–5
Fama, Eugene, 61
far right, 92, 95, 97–116, 135–7, 140, 142–5, 147–8, 153–60, 162, 164–5
fascism, 5, 6, 15, 87, 98–9, 121, 122, 135
Federal Aviation Authority, 33
Federal Election Commission, 25
Federal Reserve Bank, 41, 48, 55
Feher, Michel, 43
female suffrage, 5, 120, 122–3
feminism, 11, 93, 117, 152–3, 159, 161–2
Fidesz, 98, 100, 107, 137, 153
financial crisis (2008), 25, 32, 41–65, 74, 138, 142, 159
financial markets, 42–65, 68–9, 74–5, 77, 81, 140–1, 142
financial regulation, 41–65, 74, 83, 88, 104–5, 140–1, 142
financial sector, 22, 24–5, 32, 41–65, 74–5, 83, 88, 140–1

see also banks
financial transactions tax, 54
Finland, 92
firearms, 100, 102–3
fiscal autonomy, 67–8, 74
fiscal federalism, 67, 74
food sector, 30, 34, 58
Forza Italia, 11
France, 25, 33, 43, 67–8, 73, 74, 87, 92, 95, 96, 126–7, 128, 165
see also Front National (FN)
France, Pierre, 25
France Insoumise, La, 95, 96
Franco, Francisco, 99
free-floating capital, 46
Freiheitliche Partei Österreichs (FPÖ; Austria), 98, 108–9
Front National (FN; France), 95, 107
funding
   political, 10, 25, 26–7, 49, 73, 108
   research, 26–7, 62–3
Futuristi (Italy), 99

Gazprom, 35
gender, 92–3, 98–9, 101–2, 104, 108, 122–4, 131, 133, 137, 152–3, 161–5
General Agreement on Tariffs and Trade (GATT), 87
Germany, 5, 25, 32, 35, 43, 52, 67–75, 78–9, 83–7, 93, 95–6, 99, 106–7, 134–5, 165
gilets jaunes, 100
Giuliani, Rudy, 145
Givens, Terri, 164–5

globalization, 6–7, 41, 86–9, 94, 104, 118, 133, 135, 142, 155, 161, 165
Goldman Sachs, 58, 78
governments
  bank bailouts by, 52–3, 55, 56
  debts *see* public debt
  keenness to attract investment, 46, 59
  lobbying of *see* lobbying
  and neoliberalism, 7, 28–40, 141, 142
  outsourcing by, 29, 36–8, 141
  reach of reduced by globalization, 6–7, 118
  regulation by *see* regulation
  relationship to central banks, 148–9
  relationship to corporations, 7, 28–9, 31–40, 65, 141, 142
  relationship to the financial sector, 46, 52–60
  revolving door personnel movements, 35, 58, 60
  role in maintaining competition, 28, 30
  spending *see* public spending
  use of private sector consultants, 34–5
Great Depression, 42, 52
Greece, 72, 73, 75–81, 95–6, 107, 128, 135, 140
green movements *see* environmentalism
Greenspan, Alan, 41, 50
Guardian, 36
gun control, 100, 102–3

Halliburton, 35
Hans Böckler Stiftung, 83
Hansard Society, 115
Harteveld, Eelco, 92
hate crimes, 100
Havel, Václav, 151
Hayek, Friedrich von, 84–5, 140, 146–7
healthcare, 5, 26, 35, 36, 52
hedge funds, 47–8, 54–5, 58
  see also financial crisis (2008)
Hitler, Adolf, 5, 52, 69, 93, 99
Holy Roman Empire, 99
home repossessions, 53
homophobia, 101, 108
homosexuality, 101, 108, 124
Hungary, 58, 96, 98, 99–100, 106–7, 108, 137, 147, 149, 153

immigration, 92–4, 96–7, 104–5, 108–11, 129–30, 134–5, 143, 156–7, 160–1, 165
imperfect competition, 29–34
India, 96
indigenous peoples, 101
industrial disputes, 121, 129
inequality *see* economic inequality
inflation, 67–9, 74, 75, 77, 148
information technology (IT) sector, 30–1, 35, 45, 48–9, 58
infrastructure, 73, 74, 76
institutions
  democratic, 3, 16–17, 89, 117, 136, 150

Index

independent of democracy, 14, 82–3, 85, 101, 105–7, 114–17, 139–40, 143–4, 146–50, 155
transnational, 84–5, 92, 104, 105
interest rates, 59, 70, 71, 72, 148
international cooperation, 57, 86–8, 93, 94, 104, 105, 111, 137, 143, 155
International Institute for Finance (IIF), 75, 77, 79
International Life Sciences Institute, 34, 62–3
International Monetary Fund (IMF), 24–5, 50, 75–82, 86, 89, 142
internationalism, 104, 133
interpersonal tasks, 134, 164
Interserve, 37
Iraq, 35
Ireland, 46, 75, 96, 121, 135
Islam, 93, 98, 108–9, 146, 162
Islamic State, 98
Islamism, 98, 103, 135, 138, 146
Italy, 5, 6, 9–12, 33, 58, 71–3, 77–81, 87, 95–6, 99, 100, 103, 107–11, 127, 135, 140

Japan, 33
Jobbik, 99–100
John XXIII, 124
Johnson, Lyndon B., 131
Johnson, Simon, 25
journalism, 20, 144–5, 149, 158–9
see also media

Judaism, 93, 99–100, 107, 130, 131
judiciary, 14, 96, 105–6, 107, 110, 112, 116, 147–8

Kaczyński, Jarosław, 107
Kastner, Lisa, 54
Kennedy, John F., 131
Keynes, John Maynard, 68
Keynesianism, 40, 68–9, 74, 81, 148
Kitschelt, Herbert, 134
knowledge, 13, 38, 62–5, 144–6, 149, 157–8
see also expertise
Koch brothers, 26–7
Korea, 33
Krippner, Greta, 58
Kyenge, Cécile, 110

labour market regulation, 75
Labour Party (UK), 96, 131, 132
labour rights, 5, 137, 163
law, 14, 39, 43, 49, 111–14, 147, 149
see also courts; judiciary
Le Pen, Marine, 107
Leave.EU, 146
see also Brexit
Lega, La, 95, 100, 109–11, 127, 137
Lehman Brothers, 52
Lenin, Vladimir, 16
liberalism, 11–16, 92, 102, 104, 108, 123, 125, 130–4, 137–9, 148, 155, 160
Lincoln, Abraham, 130
lobbying, 20–2, 25, 32, 34–6,

38, 41, 43, 49, 54, 60, 65, 141
Long-Term Capital Management (LTCM), 47–8, 50
Lucano, Domenico, 110

McCarthy, Joe, 21
MacLean, Nancy, 27, 104
Macron, Emanuel, 95, 100
manada, la, 162
management consultancy, 47, 49
manufacturing industry, 96, 142, 164
market neoliberalism, 31, 32
market research, 10
markets
 and competition, 28, 29–34, 39, 63
 currency markets, 42–3, 70–1, 77, 86
 distorted markets, 61, 62
 ease of entry and exit, 29–30, 63
 financial markets, 42–65, 68–9, 74–5, 77, 81, 140–1, 142
 and globalization, 41
 and legitimation 39
 liberal preference for, 13
 and neoliberalism, 31, 32
 perfect markets, 28, 29–31, 36, 60
 and public services, 36–8
 rational markets hypothesis, 61
 secondary markets, 44–5, 53–4, 57, 59, 61, 81, 141
 stock markets, 44, 57, 61
Marx, Karl, 15–16

masculism, 92, 94, 161–2, 165
Max Planck Institute for the Study of Societies, 25
May, Theresa, 100, 112–13
media, 11, 20, 64, 73, 112, 144–6, 149, 156–7, 158–9
 see also journalism; social media
Mény, Yves, 101
Mercer, Robert, 27, 114
Merkel, Angela, 78
Merkel, Wolfgang, 39
Mexico, 100
middle classes, 133–4
mining, 96, 129, 142
Mishkin, Frederic, 48
monarchy, 15, 19
monopolies, 28, 30–1, 33, 38, 65, 144
moral hazard, 32, 57
mortgages, 46–7, 51–2, 53, 57, 61
Mounk, Jascha, 101
Movimento Cinque Stelle (M5S), 95, 110, 111
Müller, Jens-Werner, 101
Multi Fibre Agreement, 72
Mussolini, Benito, 5, 99

Napoleon, 99
national sovereignty, 86, 92, 150
National Union of Mineworkers, 129
nationalism, 52, 58, 95, 99–100, 103–4, 106–8, 118, 133–7, 142–3, 153–4
Nazism, 5, 15, 69, 84, 99, 108, 122

Index

neoclassical economics, 29–30
neoliberalism
  and competition, 28, 29–34, 39, 85
  corporate, 31–2, 39–40
  and corporation-government relations, 7, 28–9, 31–40, 141, 142
  and corruption, 19–20, 28–38, 141, 142
  and economic inequality, 19, 22–8, 32, 137, 138, 142, 153
  and education, 158
  and the environment, 160–1
  and Eurozone bailout conditions, 75–7, 140
  and financial deregulation, 41–56, 84–5, 104–5, 138, 140–1
  market, 31, 32
  neoliberal parties, 154
  and New Public Management, 29, 34–6, 39–40
  and outsourcing of public services, 29, 36–8, 141
  and regulation, 33, 41–56, 141
  rise of, 22, 139–40
  as threat to democracy, 139–43
  and the undermining of values, 141
  in the United States, 33, 34–6, 43, 104–5, 131, 142
neo-Nazism, 100
Netherlands, 92, 96, 128, 135
network externality, 30–1

New Public Management (NPM), 29, 34–6, 39–40
North Atlantic Treaty Organization (NATO), 104, 107
Northern Rock, 51–2
Norway, 92, 96, 108, 113
nostalgia *see* pessimistic nostalgia

Obama, Barack, 35, 36, 54, 142
Oesch, Daniel, 133–4, 164
oil exploration, 35
Olson, Mancur, 23–4
opinion manipulation, 26–8, 114, 144–6, 156–7, 165
Opus Dei, 99
Orbán, Viktor, 100, 106–7, 109, 136
ordoliberalism, 84–5
Organization for Economic Cooperation and Development (OECD), 22–3, 50–1, 77, 86, 89, 142
organizational tasks, 134
Österreichische Volkspartei (ÖVP), 108, 153
outsourcing, 29, 36–8, 141
Oxford Internet Institute, 28

Pabst, Adrian, 14
parliamentary sovereignty, 111–12
Pennacchi, Laura, 141
people's democracy *see* democracy, people's
perfect markets, 28, 29–31, 36, 60
pessimistic nostalgia, 91–117,

123, 131–6, 139, 142–3, 151, 153–7, 160, 161, 164–5
pharmaceutical industry, 30, 36, 58, 76
Phillips, Jess, 162
Piketty, Thomas, 21–2
Pinochet, Augusto, 39
platform companies, 30–1
pluralism, 21–2, 23–4
Podemos Unidos, 95
Poland, 58, 96, 100, 107, 147, 149
political debate, 3–4, 13–14, 16, 20–1, 89, 95, 141, 147
political funding *see* funding, political
political identities, 7–8, 106, 117, 118–38, 154, 160
political influence
 and corporations, 24–5, 31–2, 34–6, 65
 and religion, 105
 and wealth, 19, 22–8, 65
political opposition, 16, 17, 20, 100, 108, 116
political participation, 4–5, 8–10, 24
political parties
 core constituencies, 10, 126
 and corruption, 20
 decline in clarity of position, 10
 decline in memberships, 9–10, 125
 decline of trust in, 158
 election campaigns, 1–2, 10, 25, 49, 108
 funding, 10, 25, 26–7, 49, 73, 108
 marketing approaches, 10, 126, 145–6
 in opposition *see* political opposition
 and political identities, 7–8, 106, 119–32, 136, 154
 as representative of citizens' interests, 12–13, 119–20
 and social movements, 151–66
politicians
 distance from mass supporters, 6, 10, 118–19, 125–6
 relations with business elites, 6, 10, 25, 41, 140–1, 142
 and trustworthiness, 125–6
 see also government; political parties
populism, 5, 11, 26, 28, 62, 91, 94–7, 101–2, 105, 108, 115–17, 135, 137, 140, 143–5, 147
Portugal, 6, 72, 87, 96, 99, 127, 135–6
post-industrialism, 2, 8
'post-' phenomena, 2–3
post-truth, 145–6, 158
power, 7, 14, 22, 116, 143, 147
Prague Spring (1968), 151
Prawo i Sprawiedliwość (PiS; Poland), 100, 107
precarious employment, 163, 164
press *see* journalism; media
privatization, 29, 36–8, 76, 141
progressive taxation, 5, 89, 104, 133

Index

protectionism, 57, 142
protest voting, 12
public debt, 52–3, 59–60, 66–7, 74–83, 148
public opinion, 59, 64, 115
public–private initiatives, 141
public services, 29, 32, 34, 36–8, 52, 53, 141, 164
public spending, 52–3, 59, 67, 68–9, 75, 77, 82, 148, 163
Putin, Vladimir, 107

race, 98, 102, 103, 104, 110, 122, 130–1
see also ethnic minorities
racism, 110, 135
see also xenophobia
Rackete, Carola, 110–11
Rajan, Raghuram, 50
rape, 161–2
rational markets hypothesis, 61
Reagan, Ronald, 85
redistributive taxation, 5, 89, 104, 133
referenda, 12, 78, 79, 80, 112–14
refugees, 107, 108, 109–11, 135, 156–7
regulation
  corporate regulation, 7, 26–7, 33, 39, 141
  deregulation, 41–65, 74, 83, 104–5, 140–1
  financial regulation, 41–65, 74, 83, 88, 104–5, 140–1, 142
  and global trade, 86
  labour market regulation, 75
  and neoliberalism, 33, 41–56, 141
  regulatory capture, 54, 62–3
  safety regulation, 33
regulatory capture, 54, 62–3
Rehm, Philipp, 134
religion, 6, 7–8, 9–10, 15, 92–3, 96, 98, 101, 102, 104–5, 118, 120–36, 158
Renzi, Matteo, 12
Republican Party, 17, 26, 102, 105, 106, 130–1, 137, 153
République En Marche, La (France), 95
research and development, 44
research funding see funding, research
research institutes, 26–7, 34, 62–3
revolutions, 15, 121, 122
revolving door system, 35, 58, 60
risk sharing, 45, 46, 47, 55
Russia/Soviet Union, 15–17, 27–8, 35, 45, 48, 57, 96, 106–8, 114, 122, 144, 154

safety regulation, 33
Salazar, António de Oliveira, 99
Salvini, Matteo, 100, 107, 109–11, 147
Scandinavia, 5, 87, 92, 135
see also Denmark; Finland; Norway; Sweden
Scargill, Arthur, 129
Schröder, Gerhard, 35
Schweizerische Volkspartei (SVP; Switzerland), 109

science, 13, 34, 103, 125, 144–5, 149, 160
Sea Watch, 110–11
Second Vatican Council, 124
Second World War, 5, 15, 52, 69, 122, 135
secondary legislation, 112–13
secondary markets, 44–5, 53–4, 57, 59, 61, 81, 141
secularization, 8, 125
self-employment, 76, 164
services sector, 124, 161
sexuality, 93, 98, 101, 104, 108, 124, 131, 133, 137, 153
shareholder value maximization, 43–4, 51, 141, 142
Shiller, Robert, 61
shipping industry, 30, 73, 81
slavery, 130
Slovakia, 96, 107
Slovenia, 9, 96, 107
social class, 6, 7–8, 9–10, 15–16, 96, 118, 120–36, 152–3, 162–3
social democracy *see* democracy, social
Social Democratic Party (Denmark), 96
social enterprise, 36–7
Social Enterprise UK, 36
social media, 26–8, 95, 114, 117, 144, 146, 149, 156–7, 158, 165
social movements, 21, 81, 91, 94–5, 151–66
social policies, 86
socialism, 5, 11, 15–17, 19–20, 72, 106, 107, 121, 123, 129, 136, 139, 155

Soros, George, 106–7
South Africa, 17–18
sovereignty
  economic, 86
  national, 86, 92, 150
  parliamentary, 111–12
Soviet Union *see* Russia/Soviet Union
Spain, 6, 9, 46, 72, 73, 74–5, 87, 95, 99, 127, 134, 135–6, 162
Stalin, Josef, 16
state socialism, 15–17, 19–20, 72, 106, 107, 122, 136, 151
statist capitalism, 33
statistical services, 149
Steenvoorden, Eefje, 92
stock markets, 44, 57, 61
Streeck, Wolfgang, 39, 59, 85–6
stress tests, 55
strikes, 121, 129
student debt, 158
sub-prime mortgages, 51–2, 53, 57, 61
Surel, Yves, 101
Susskind, Jamie, 27
Sweden, 61, 92, 96, 108, 128, 134
Swedish Central Bank, 61
Switzerland, 9, 92, 96, 108, 109, 134
Syriza (Greece), 78, 81, 95–6

tariffs, 72, 86–7, 88
tax evasion, 76
taxation
  of corporations, 7, 22–3, 46, 155

and demand management, 68–9
evasion of, 76
financial transactions tax, 54
in Greece, 73, 75, 76, 81
redistributive, 5, 89, 104, 133
relation to public spending and debt, 59, 67, 68–9, 74, 75, 81, 82, 148
and returns on wealth, 22–3
tax rate competition, 7, 46, 88
Tea Party movement (US), 26–7
technical tasks, 134
television, 11, 145
terrorism, 98, 103, 135, 138, 156
textile industry, 71, 72
Thatcher, Margaret, 85
think-tanks, 26–7
Third Way politics, 58
tolerance, 13, 104
'too big to fail' organizations, 32, 37, 55, 63, 79
Toozetelevision, Adam, 41, 43
trade, 86–8, 104–5, 142
trade unions, 23, 75, 80, 83, 142, 158, 163–4
transnational corporations *see* corporations
transnational institutions, 84–5, 92, 104, 105
transsexuality, 124
'troika', 75–82
true markets *see* perfect markets
Trump, Donald, 25, 27, 35, 54, 57, 87–8, 92, 100, 102–8, 142, 144–5, 147, 153–4, 161
trustworthiness, 125–6, 158
Turkey, 96, 113

UK Independence Party (UKIP), 162
unemployment, 52, 53, 148
United Kingdom
alt.right, 111, 114–15, 162
corporate governance, 43
election campaigns, 1–2, 114
and the Eurozone crisis, 80
and the financial crisis, 46, 51–2, 60
financial deregulation, 43, 46, 51–2, 60
hate crimes, 100
imperialism, 98, 111
lack of written constitution, 111–16
miners' strike, 129
neoliberalism, 36–7, 43, 85
outsourcing of public services, 36–7
parliamentary sovereignty, 111–12
pessimistic nostalgia, 92, 96, 98, 100, 111–16, 143, 162
political identities, 120, 127, 128, 129, 132
populism, 96
rejects international cooperation, 57
revolving door system, 35
suffrage, 120
see also Bank of England; Brexit; Conservative Party (UK)

Index

United Nations, 104
United States
  abortion legislation, 162
  alt.right, 100, 102–6, 107, 108, 142, 144–5, 153, 154
  and the Bretton Woods arrangement, 42–3, 69–70
  climate change denial, 88, 103, 145, 159–60
  Constitution, 25, 105
  corporate political lobbying, 24–5, 26–7, 34, 36
  corporate governance, 43
  corporate regulation, 33
  democratic moments, 5, 122
  democratic pluralism, 21, 24
  economic inequality, 21–2
  electoral turnout, 17
  and the financial crisis, 41, 49–50, 52–4, 57, 58, 60–1
  financial deregulation, 41, 42–3, 49–50, 54, 58, 60–1, 142
  gun control, 100, 102–3
  immigration, 104–5, 129–30
  neoliberalism, 33, 34–6, 43, 104–5, 131, 142
  new public management, 34–6
  pessimistic nostalgia, 92, 96, 100, 102–6, 129–32, 142, 153
  political identities, 122, 129–32
  populism, 96, 105, 144–5
  potential vote tampering, 17
  protectionism, 57, 142
  race, 102, 103, 104, 122, 130–1
  rejection of international cooperation, 57, 88
  religion, 129–31
  revolving door system, 58, 60
  suffrage, 122
  Supreme Court, 25, 105
  Tea Party movement, 26–7
  Trump presidency *see* Trump, Donald
universal suffrage, 5, 7–8, 121–2, 124
universalism, 96, 133

vaccination, 103, 145
values, 3, 93, 98, 104–7, 131, 137, 141, 143, 151, 155–8, 160, 164–5
van Bijsterveld, Sophie, 150
Vatican, 99, 124
Vauchez, Antoine, 25
Venezuela, 147
venture capitalism, 55
violence, 5, 16, 97–101, 103, 108, 115, 121, 137, 143, 156, 161–2
vote tampering, 17
voter turnout, 8–9, 17–18, 84, 106, 125, 126
Vox, 162

Wall Street collapse, 52
wealth
  and clandestine opinion manipulation, 26–8, 114, 144–6, 156–7, 165

and collective action, 23–4, 26
and control of knowledge, 62–5, 144, 149
created by financial markets, 45, 47, 50
and economic returns, 22–3
influence on science and journalism, 149
and lobbying, 25, 65
and pessimistic nostalgia, 144
and political funding, 25, 26–7
and political influence, 19, 22–8, 65
redistribution of, 5, 23, 89, 133, 134
and taxation, 22–3
Welch, Stephen, 3
welfare state, 5, 104, 133, 135, 137, 141
working classes, 15–16, 96, 121, 122, 129, 131–3, 136, 152–3
World Bank, 86, 89
WorldCom, 49–50
World Trade Organization (WTO), 87, 89, 104

xenophobia, 11, 28, 88, 92–5, 99–100, 102, 108–10, 115, 135–7, 152–5, 159

yellow vests *see gilets jaunes*
Yugoslavia, 15